My Journey with Prisoners:

PERCEPTIONS, OBSERVATIONS, AND OPINIONS

by
Carol E. Briney, MLS, FAFA, AAFA, TS

August 2013

An essay submitted to
Kent State University
in partial fulfillment of the requirements
for the Master of Liberal Studies degree

Approved by

Dr. Manacy Pai
    Adviser

Dr. Clare L. Stacey
    Reader

Dr. Richard M. Berrong
    Director of Liberal Studies

Dr. Raymond A. Craig
    Dean, College of Arts and Sciences

ISBN-10:0984297685
ISBN-13:978-0-9842976-8-9

Graphic Design and Typography by
Daniel Szwedko Graphics

Photography by David Bradshaw and
Benjamin Lehman

Printed in the United States

Available through www.Amazon.com,
Seattle, WA, or directly from Publisher

Contact Information:

Reentry Bridge Network, Inc., Publisher
P. O. Box 9491
Canton, OH 44711
www.ReentryBridgeNetwork.org

"Carol Briney's explanation of the techniques she has developed over the years to deal with the problems experienced by the male prison population and their transition back into the outside world is both fascinating and important. Rather than setting off with the latest sociological or psychological theories and developing treatments in a void, she has derived all her methods "the old-fashioned way," speaking with the prisoners themselves constantly to see what works and what does not work, what explains their behavior and what does not. The result, written in a direct, sometimes amusing, but always jargon-free style, is sure to intrigue and astound. It is sure to convince you that she has, indeed, discovered things that everyone involved with male prisoners needs to know."

   - **Dr. Richard M. Berrong,** Director, Master of Liberal Studies Program, Kent State University

"In this work, Carol Briney gives a human face to the statistics about mass incarceration in the United States. As readers, we are asked to think critically about the way in which our communities and social policies foster crime and recidivism. Most importantly, Briney shows us the importance of education for prisoner health and well-being and suggests that we cannot solve the problems associated with incarceration until we heal the minds and psyches of inmates. An inspirational and challenging read!"

   - **Dr. Clare Stacey**

"With this book Briney takes us behind the scenes of prisons. Focusing on the experiences of the men in prison, Briney talks about what it takes to reform the mind of the man behind bars. She discusses the psychosocial and spiritual programs through which male prisoners learn how to make sense of their lives, cultivate a sense of purpose, and come to realize their sense of worth. This renewed ability to focus on self is what Briney says ultimately is likely to prevent these men from committing crimes again and will help them in their efforts to integrate into the mainstream society."

- **Dr. Manacy Pai**

"It takes community to reduce recidivism."

- **Carol E. Briney**

TABLE OF CONTENTS

ACKNOWLEDGEMENTS

This essay is written as partial fulfillment of my Masters of Liberal Studies. I am often asked what motivated me to pursue my degree at the age of sixty-one and I almost always share the following two events as my answer.

First, I recall the morning that I drove through blowing snow for two and a half hours to the central office of Ohio Department of Rehabilitation and Corrections (ODRC) in Columbus, to meet with Toni Brooks, the Director of Prisons, and Dr. Ed Rhine, the Director of Reentry. The purpose of the meeting was to discuss onsite reentry initiative programs for prisoners.

Just a week before, Toni arranged for me to make my inaugural trip to a female prison to facilitate a two-day workshop on the art of handmade books. Those two days left me feeling as if I'd been thrown into a pond of piranha, and I'd spent my entire travel time convincing myself not to tell Toni how I truly felt about my experience. I was equally rattled by the fact that I had no solutions to offer. If I am going to be critical of a scenario, I like to offer up solutions. In this case, I had nothing to offer. I vowed to evade the issue if asked.

As I entered the conference room, Toni took one look at me and said, "Tell me about the women's camp." I tried to dance around it. But when I slipped up on her third inquiry and answered "Well, it was different from the men," she took pen in hand, drew her yellow tablet closer and asked "How so?" Ed also drew his pen and tablet closer. I had no way out now but to disclose all that I had experienced.

After 20 minutes of spilling my story, I quietly but anxiously sat back in my seat. Toni's glance shifted from the tablet where she had been taking copious notes, and she softly asked, "Is that it?" I answered "I think so." Toni and Ed put their pens down, sat up straight, looked at each other, and Toni called her assistant into the conference room. Counting in the air with her fingers, Toni began to quickly give him multiple directives. After she dismissed him, she turned and gazed at me a minute before she said, "You have given me more information in twenty minutes than my entire staff has in twenty-five years. I've been telling people that our approach to working with female prisoners has to be different than with the males. They always told me that I was biased cause I'm a female. You just gave me six critical answers. Now I know what to do about situations I didn't know what to do with just twenty minutes ago. Thank you."

To say I was perplexed and surprised would be an understatement. I just sat there and all I could meekly offer was "I wasn't going to tell you any of that. I didn't want to come across stereotypical or judgmental."

"So, what's the answer to all of this?" she asked, sitting back in her chair and again gazing at me.

"I don't know. That's why I didn't want to give you my real report because I haven't come up with any solutions. None. I have nothing." I remember feeling at such a loss.

"Well, you will. You will come up with the solution, and I need you to promise to bring it to me as soon as you do. In fact, I need you to promise us that you will never hold back on your observations or opinions. You have great insight, and we need you to talk to us. Promise me?"

Well, it took me two years, but I now know the answer to Toni's question. It is found in the theories of play therapy and the healing attributes of dirt and water.

Female prisoners need to work inside greenhouses, raise earthworms, and recycle garbage to compost. The dirt heals children who didn't receive nurturing as babies and toddlers. The water heals the wounds of sexual abuse. The worms provide life for the innate female nesting behavior. The structure of planting seeds - watering them correctly, not uncovering their dirt to see if they sprouted, following the process exactly until the prisoner is able to actually eat the tomato that she grew - will grow trust. That trust will grow in many things: self, systems, nature, peers and happy endings.

The second motivating event occurred two weeks after I met with Toni and Ed. I was on an airplane coming back from New Mexico just after Christmas. I was feeling particularly old and stagnant as I sat waiting for the other passengers to board.

Staring at the front of the plane, wondering who would be sitting by my window, I noticed a very tall, thin, elderly black man finding his way down the aisle. He wore a drab green parka similar to the homeless I knew. Counting rows with his hands, he stopped beside me. I stood up for him to slide into his spot. Having noticed he sat down on his seatbelt I told him if he would rise up just a little, I'd pull it out from under him. As we worked together to recover the belt and get it fastened around him, he proceeded to tell me that he was 95 years old, legally blind, and had just come from a big family reunion in Atlanta. He was headed home to Cleveland. He was also hard of hearing, so conversation was quite limited between us. I could feel his energy. He had fifteen family members on our plane, but his independence evidently kept them from monitoring him too tightly. I was amused. This man had spent 95 years in Cleveland and was articulate, gracious, and very educated. He was an outlier. I so desired to quiz him. He was born at the turn of the century, and I longed to motivate myself with his stories of overcoming. But, I recognized my voice wouldn't carry well enough in the noisy plane for him to hear me sufficiently. All I could do was to wonder and watch over him as he napped on our long flight home.

The infant grandson I had visited in Albuquerque would be 35 when I reached this man's age. I had an entire life ahead of me. And, I had people who wanted to work closely with me to resolve social ills that lead to generational poverty and incarceration.

Those are the two events that catapulted me into graduate school. The people and events who inspired and awoke me to the fact that I needed to go back to the university and earn my master's degree. I am very grateful to them and for the awareness that I would need more education for the journey that lie ahead.

I must also acknowledge and express gratitude to my family for allowing me to drag them through my process. Falicia and Brittney, my adopted granddaughters, got uprooted and moved from New Mexico to Ohio during formative years. Alicia, my daughter, thought that I had lost my mind. Jake, my grandson, did not get time to hang around with his eccentric Nanny. Hopefully they have seen some of the good that has come from my journey. And kudos to my nephew, Clinton Dean Kifolo, who had a great influence on our move to Ohio.

Additionally, there are many professors from Central New Mexico College, University of New Mexico, and Kent State University who have impacted my life with both knowledge and generous friendship and guidance. Most especially I must thank professors Manacy Pai, Clare Stacey, Richard Berrong, John Stalvey, Richard Serpe, and my long-time friends Mary Bates-Ulibarri and Dr. Stephen Schoonmaker.

Special thanks to the many volunteers, especially Andrea Krommes and David Bradshaw, who have taught with me inside the prisons. And thank you to the ODRC staff who graciously supported and guided our endeavors onsite: Khellah Konteh, Dennis Baker, Richard Hall, Carla Bernard, Marie Holland, Ed Rhine, Bennie Kelly, and Jerry Spatney. ODRC Directors Terry Collins, Ernie Moore, Gary Mohr, and Assistant Directors Mike Randle and Steven Huffman. Ohio Federal Public Defender Dennis Terez has also walked with me inside the prisons and in community.

Last but certainly not least, there are fifty thousand adults living inside Ohio prisons. I have had the opportunity to get to know thousands of them and count many as my friends. They know who they are and why their names can't be listed here. I also include the hundreds of national prisoners who have corresponded with me through writings and art over the years. They have been kind to me, and it is through their honesty, transparency, friendship and trust that I have been able to take this journey and arrive at the thoughts that I share in these writings. "Namaste. Be safe."

And, to my readers, thank you for taking time to read and consider my perceptions, observations and opinions with an open mind. It takes community to reduce recidivism.

                                    - Carol E. Briney

DISCLAIMER

Many people will read this essay - victims of crime, corrections staff, former prisoners, current prisoners, and family members. The majority will be civilians who may not have given much forethought to the culture or challenges of incarceration. Whoever you are, I feel compelled to ask you to read the essay as a whole, including the following statement.

I walked into the world of corrections with no preconceived ideas about prisons or prisoners. I had never been victimized nor did I have any concept of the struggles of poverty. In hindsight, I was superficial and naïve. I was drafted into this purposeful life. I accepted the invitation to participate because it promised to be an interesting and fun experience. However, once I stepped into the arena and had the veil ripped from my shallow world, I found people whose needs called to my mind and soul without cessation – they called louder than my own needs. I quickly learned I don't know how to not do this work.

I realize my perceptions, observations, and opinions are based on my own experiences as I've walked through this journey amidst prisoners. I have worked hard to be able to catch glimpses of the world through their eyes, through their experiences, so I could continue to seek out and write program curriculum that would help us as a society to break the horrific negative generational cycles that claim the lives of our children, the hearts of our families, and the future of our nation.

My compassion and prayers go out to the victims and families who have known great loss; families of the prisoners who also have known great loss; volunteers, interns, and staff who have worked inside prisons and found themselves lost in the deviation or innate aggressiveness, or been reminded of their own victimization; those who have known great loss as a result of vicarious traumas; and to the prisoners.

Praise and prayers go out to the individuals who see the needs of humanity as a whole and strive with loving care to heal the damage by nurturing individuals as they journey through the dark night of the souls and struggle to find their light.

I apologize now to anyone who may feel offended or misjudged in this writing. I can only hope my words have brought you some worthy consideration. I can only write from the pathways that I have traveled. Anything less would be wasted words. Thank you for this consideration.

METHODOLOGY

The purpose of this essay is to concisely capture perceptions, observations and opinions from my decade-long work of writing and facilitating programs with prisoners. I did not set out to write a book; I simply began this journey with one foot in front of the other, never quite sure about the next step. There were no formal preparations or processes such as going through the Institutional Review Board; I knew nothing about that.

My methodology was to simply walk with the prisoners and ask them ongoing questions about their populations, history, cases, and to discover their opinions as to what might change negative life cycles, generational incarceration, and recidivism. From that information, I would write programs that we would implement together. The questions took form with and along the journey. There was no formal, preconceived set of questions. Without the progress of the journey, the questions would not have surfaced. However, I am an older, educated, middle class, white woman from the Midwest and I had not previously been immersed in the cultures of poverty, so it was all new to me. I think reality and my enthusiasm to embrace a totally new environment blessed me with an "eyes wide open" posture through which to examine, question, and seek solutions to the stirrings of poverty, incarceration, and other subcultures.

The demographics of the prison students were full-range with regard to race, age, religion, education, social class, years of incarceration, number of prison stints, and criminal charges. Other than one-weekend workshop at a female prison, my interaction was exclusively with male prisoners. There were numerous prisoners who were born in countries outside of the United States, most of which had English as their second language. My interactions with staff included both male and female. My experiences in community included the full-spectrum of family members and ex-prisoners, male and female, who had reentered community.

At the end of each class cycle, we would meet with the students and brainstorm on what worked and what did not. Then we would change and adjust programs to better fit the prisoners' needs. I taught about half of the classes, along with guest speakers, interns, and volunteers, and prisoners taught the remaining half. I was, and am, deeply immersed in the prison population, as much as I can be without actually living there. There's no other staff inside the classrooms with me, so I am privileged to a lot of "truth-telling" and sharing.

I am obsessed with solving the riddles of social ills. I seek the secrets of successful habilitation and rehabilitation. Every minute inside a prison brings new insights, thoughts, questions, and opportunities to seek out and test solutions. My methodology is to continuously build on acquired first-hand knowledge from experiences, stories, events, and results. It also involves continuously searching through more current multi-discipline writings and many hours of hashing and rehashing ideas with like minds. Always, the most important information comes from prisoners or ex-prisoners. It is rare for me to discover any writing or theories that really make sense inside prisons. When I do, I contact the author and often bring them into the prison, most of whom have already spent time with the population.

I will add here - hoping this statement will not be viewed as me being controversial - just because a person has been on staff in a correctional setting does not mean they have knowledge of effective solutions. More often than not, under these conditions, their prejudices, biases, training, and "good-old boy" behavior for co-worker acceptance have rendered them part of the problem. They have compromised their humanity and reconstructed their thoughts and emotions in order to survive long-term employment inside prison walls. In other words, it is easier to oppress a people whom one sees as less than human. This reframe can alter all the day-to-day rules of interaction, but not one's karmic beliefs. This causes gradual self-destruction.

Chapter One
WELCOME TO PRISON

I knew nothing more about prisons or
prisoners than the average Jane on the
middle-class streets, when my cousin, Roy,
phoned me at midnight and asked me to
critique the art and writings of prisoners from
across America. With many question marks
above my head and a sincerely aggravated
tone in my voice, I simply replied into the
phone "What?" I needed nothing more to do
in my standard allotment of 24x7. But, there
it was: an invitation to enter a new frontier
and to further saddle my mule of mounting
tasks.

I argued, using as many of my resistant
coping skills as I could pull out of my
exhausted, chaotic mind. But, the intrigue
and call of something new and uncharted
was just enough to tilt the scales in Roy's

favor. "Well, only if they are serious! I'm not looking for a relationship or a pen pal. Make sure they understand that."

Roy printed a two inch ad in his national prisoner newsletter, inviting prisoners to submit art and writing to me for critique, and the rest is history.

It wasn't too far into the process that I found myself sitting in the living room at midnight, with stacks of manuscripts, poetry, and art, all waiting for critiques. Beside these stacks were the stacks of my own unfinished canvases, manuscript, and housework. All I had seemed to accomplish was to grow my sense of being overwhelmed, which fed my crankiness towards my girls. I realized I had to find a responsible way out from underneath the mountain of commitment that was beginning to devour my ration of sleep.

So I sat and pondered how to satisfy this commitment. I knew every submission came with the hope that I could and would connect the individual with publishers and galleries. I began to brainstorm how I could reverse the connection process and land all of the materials in front of the public in one fell swoop, and be done with it. That is, thinking that I would be done with it; not yet knowing anything about the personality traits and tenacity of male prisoners.

After many looping thoughts regarding my predicament, I stumbled upon the idea of publishing anthologies that retained the original presentations of the art, poetry, and stories. I could call it <u>The Prison Coffee Table Book Project</u> and fund it with grants. With that epiphany, I issued a formal press release for Roy's prison newsletter, inviting more materials to be sent to me for publishing. The stockpile grew quickly and I set out to bring the anthology to fruition – a task which took three years of intense research and development.

The ink was barely dry on the press release, when the idea of the project reached an Ohio prison: Grafton Correctional Institution (GCI). I was invited to fly two thousand miles and hold a four-day fine arts workshop with eighty-three male prisoners. Well, I had no preconceived ideas as to what that experience would look or feel like. I just knew I was compelled to fulfill this invitation and walk through yet another gate to this new frontier. It was as if something took hold of me and not only could I not break free from it, I had no desire to try. I was simply rushing with the flow. This was so obvious, that a friend wrote me a check for ten thousand dollars to finance the trip.

Here is my account of that experience. It was written right after my return home from GCI a little more than seven years ago. Keep in mind I did not know any prisoners, nor had I ever been inside a prison when I entered GCI for those four days. I feel it is important to include it in this text because it displays my naivety and reflects my initial observations of a prison. At this point in time, after passing through prison gates thousands of times, I would never be able to recapture that experience effectively. As a foundational and historical reference to this writing, I believe it is important I reflect the observations and perceptions of a newcomer to such an extreme and profound environment.

Four Days inside Grafton Prison

As my cousin, Roy, and I walked up to the red brick guard house on Thursday night, May 25, 2006, I really had no preconceived ideas around what to expect on the other side of the gate. Roy had said that it was going to be loud and abusive, and he was concerned about how it would affect me. He said it would be a life changing event, either positive or negative.

The young female guard on duty patiently checked in the six boxes of art and supplies we brought into GCI. We stripped the metal and jewelry off of our bodies, took off our shoes and coats and placed them in the standard plastic gray security bin. We walked silently through the metal detectors, signed our names and received our first visitor passes. Then, we proceeded through the sallyport gates and onto the prison grounds.

I paused to feel and absorb. We had indeed arrived. My heart sped and my breath was taken as my eyes acknowledged where I stood, caged in layers of razor wire. It bore a marked resemblance to the air force bases I'd traveled to with the U.S.O. during Viet Nam. Even the uniforms were the familiar blue. Roy broke our silence with a hardy "Welcome to prison."

The prison was designed like a wheel of cement spokes leading to separate buildings, with grass in between. No straight lines from one place to another. Mostly one-story buildings with flowerbeds. The only visible bars were horizontal on cell block windows. As we walked, slowly calculating the risks and surroundings, one of the prison teachers led us toward the Visitor's Center. Suddenly our small talk was interrupted from behind, "Excuse me! I'm coming through." We turned, stepped off of the sidewalk, and waited while a large guard pedaled past us on a small mountain bike. Our minds went whimsical, but we remained focused and returned to our social bantering with our escort as we continued to our destination.

As we entered the Visitors' Center, we looked up to see a handful of men, dressed in blue, entering from the other side of the building.

I had thought there would be a couple of minutes to gather myself, when I realized these men were the core group of ten prisoners who had come to meet with us, most of whom were officers of the sponsoring NAACP inmate group. My heart skipped as I turned and walked towards the men. Let it begin, my heart whispered, as I made eye contact with each individual presented to me, reading his name tag, and shaking hands in the friendship we'd established through months of mail. There was an energy of excitement that softly filled the air. We went about our business of sitting in a circle and discussing the weekend that was unfolding in front of us. Who were we, who were they, and what was expected? Who was attending, and what did the rooms look like? What supplies would the men need to bring? Lots of heads nodded up and down, smiles were free-flowing, so I figured we were on the right track for the workshops that would engulf the next three days. Then the clock hands signaled 9 P.M. The men had to leave and so did we. Everyone stood, and I instinctively hugged each one good night. Prior to our leaving, the staff sponsor took me aside and nervously told me "Do not hug the prisoners! Most of them are murderers and little to no physical contact can be made." I replied "Okay." I asked if there were any other rules I needed to be aware of since I was going into a prison for the first time. He said he was trying hard to think about that,

6

and at the moment he couldn't think of any.

The staff sponsor escorted us off the property, and we followed his car to the new Mexican food restaurant to meet his family and be their guests for dinner. That was a treat. Roy and I laughed when we saw a dictionary on the back of the menu, explaining the foods we ate daily in New Mexico. We meant to bring a menu back with us to show around, but got busy visiting and forgot. I talked with our sponsor about GCI, combat in Viet Nam, and his passion for being the pastor of a Southern Baptist Church in a northern state. And, oddly enough, both he and his wife had extensive experience in the printing and book distribution industry. We laughed at the coincidences each day brings to us. He shared how the Ohio Prison Industries (OPI) print shop was looking for work to print. All this time, Roy was at the other end of the table entertaining their young sons with magic and humor.

In deep contemplation of the next morning, we drove to the hotel. What would it be like? Roy again warned me of how awful he had seen things turn in some of his prison visits. We held tight to the words of the staff sponsor that, though he would not be there, he had hand-picked everyone who would be our security and guides for the weekend.

It was four o'clock New Mexico time when

the wakeup call rang. Jet lag and all, we
sprung out of the bed and got busy
preparing for our adventure. Eighty-three
men had signed up and gotten a pass for
the workshop. The same men would be in
all of the classes. That was good. I wouldn't
have to start over on each class, and we
could gain more ground in a continuous flow
of workshop topics. If a prisoner had not
received a pass, he could not attend. It was
Memorial Day weekend and we had been
told this was a good turnout. We were also
forewarned that ninety percent of the time,
ten minutes into a presentation, the
prisoners often stand up and walk out
because the presenters have demeaning
attitudes towards the audience. We were a
tad nervous.

The first gathering was in the chapel on
Friday morning at 7:30 A.M. It was an open
forum for Roy and I to address whatever
questions the group had about us, about art,
about the weekend program, and about the
Prison Coffee Table Book Project. The
questions were quite varied, and the room
was warm and welcoming. We were so glad
to finally be right where we were. We were
excited about the weekend together like a
child at Christmas, a new puppy, or all of that
rolled into one. We explored each other's
minds for an hour and a half and then the
Deputy Warden took us on a tour of the
facility, and on to the officers' dining room

for a quick lunch. He cordially extended the tour to the entire 2,000 acre, state-owned operation. There are four prison facilities clustered together, each with a different population profile, housing over six thousand men collectively. We toured the 2,000 acre farm and the camp facility which is a stone building that has seen a century of prisoners.

It had been raining since we left the chapel, and, by now, I was soaked. The Deputy Warden took us back to his office to wait out the few minutes before the next workshop started. He apologized for not noticing I was not prepared for rain. He then loaned me his raincoat for the weekend. We laughed about having to fly from the New Mexico desert to Ohio to experience rain, and about his Sponge Bob desk accessories. We assured him we would help him grow his collection. We laughed about the gifts people give him. He was very gracious.

The first workshop was held in the library. Prior to the men coming in, I spread out four dozen books I had brought to donate. After five years of university studies, I saw this as an opportunity to share my collection of books. The men were so excited to get to read new material pertaining to the arts, that I had to actually stack the books back up to get their attention regarding the handmade books workshop. It felt good to know my books were in a good home, where their knowledge would be studied and learned. I proceeded to talk about all of the sample handmade books I had brought with me: their uniqueness, their history, and their functionality. I could hear the gears turning as the poets and writers visualized filling the pages with their own words. The artists began designing books in their heads and illustrating them. I could see it in their eyes and hear it in their voices. It was very gratifying to have the topic so well received.

Between each workshop, Roy and I were escorted off the grounds for a two to three hour break while the men went to eat and reported back to their cell blocks to be counted. Each time, we had to go back through the security processes, always being checked and escorted. Always gracious guards.

Numerous times, Roy and I would get caught up in the moment and take off across the yard in a crowd of the students and would be called back or have to wait for a security escort. "Ms. Briney, you can't be doing that!" they would say to me. I'd laugh and keep bantering with the men who had brought questions and comments to me. I felt like Socrates walking with his students. Many questions going both ways. There was not one instance where Roy or I felt fear. We felt a tremendous amount of appreciation that had a lasting impact on us. In fact, we were all students in this experience.

The four-day weekend was comprised of some thirty hours of workshops, lectures and critiques. There were ten segments: hand-made books, print making, color theory, Frieda Kahlo style and diary, and a slide lecture on my manuscript, <u>The Retablo Affect</u>. The event concluded with a poetry slam and jazz music on Sunday night. We had rearranged our time so we could all work on closure that last night. I didn't have enough foresight to build it into the original agenda.

The theme for the entire weekend was "Seeing Things Differently." We explored ways of expressing self through multiple media. To make the art more interesting to the viewer, we talked about putting ourselves into the pictures as Frieda did. We talked about breaking through the boundaries we impose on ourselves and our thinking. We talked about getting through the garbage and seeing the God in people and in ourselves and what attributes might show up to define the spirit inside and what that person is truly all about. We focused a lot on seeing ourselves differently and being okay with our goodness, our self-expression, and our individuality. We talked about change.

While I was in the front of the room lecturing

or demonstrating hands-on work, Roy moved quietly about the room, bonding through humor. He later told me he was asked numerous times to describe what life looks like outside the walls. Some of the men had been there for over twenty-five years. They joked that it is their retirement home. Every now and then, the joke was about me and I would become the focus of a set-up that ended with us all laughing. We laughed a lot and set our intention to have fun together. The setting was playful, but, in the same breath, filled with very high energy, incredible intelligence, and unpretentious, unfiltered truth. Roy and I have since had many discussions around the telepathic energy and communication that we were allowed to experience. It was unbelievably easy and clear. I had been told about the telepathic atmosphere in prison settings, but took it lightly until I was in the midst of it. I can still hear it today.

On that Saturday morning, the fog was so thick that the yard was closed and the 7:30 workshop was cancelled shortly after we got set up for it. That meant we had to scrunch the remaining time in order to cover the entire curriculum. The corners cut meant that the hands-on time shrank. But, this group of men was so sharp and attentive that I knew they were picking it up enough through the lectures to be able to implement it themselves after we left. I made the decision to donate the book samples I had initially intended to bring home. The men would need the samples and I could make more. I was really feeling time begin to squeeze me and I knew I was going to leave feeling I didn't get enough work done with the group.

The yard was locked down for the entire two hours the workshop had been scheduled for, and the men were going to lunch afterwards. So, we had to remain inside the buildings until the yard was unlocked. This gave us a great opportunity to visit with the staff who were with us. One of the teachers took me over to the classrooms and showed me photos of the teddy bears prisoners make for traumatized children, and quilts blind prisoners make using two-inch square sticky notes to count stitches. She showed me shelves of donated craft material. Her job description was to help the prisoners complete their GED so they could go forward with their education. Her only duty was to school with books and computers; but, her passion was introducing the men to hands-on crafts that would have latent benefits of teaching them skills that would develop patience, patterns, self-expression, and give them a product they could be proud of and even sell. She loaded up a box of goodies for us to use in our book-making class. As we gathered things up, she told me stories of working in the female prisons and we cried about the children, and abused women doing time.

The second slot of time on Saturday was set aside for me to critique the men's work. They filled the general purpose rec room with everything they wanted to talk to me about, or to show us. As I stepped into the room, I felt overwhelmed and immediately realized I had to accomplish three things in the next two hours. I had to time it so I could spend time with each artist. I had to search my education for new information to challenge each one, including the very seasoned masters. And, I had to be able to critique them in such a manner as to not cause any harm, but to encourage their creativity and inspire them to reach deeper within and capture themselves, challenge them to explore new techniques, and encourage more self-expression. The latter was the most challenging for me. I actually felt nauseous as I pondered how to proceed. They were all looking at me and waiting.

They were more nervous than I. So, I decided to use my university experiences and explained how it would work in a college setting. I invited them all to follow me around to each piece of art and to hear what I would say. Doing that, they would learn from all of the critiques and scenarios. I asked their permission to proceed and stated I had no intention of embarrassing them or harming them. They swallowed and agreed. And away we went. It was great, and I surprised myself with my ability to gift something to everyone. I became more aware and confident of my own education and insight, and that was a great gift for me.

Each night I would quiz Roy and wonder whether what I had chosen for the topics would be interesting and challenging enough for these men. I was really quite unsettled about each workshop, feeling I might bore my audience. So, when the feedback was beyond my imaginings, I felt valued and encouraged.

They were hungry for any new knowledge. They told me I gave them the first real art classes they had ever had. Programs were scarce in prison. They began to bring other pieces of art into the last couple of workshops to show me what they had been doing privately, fearing peer criticism of their experiments. Now they stood proud and vowed to continue down the paths they had been curious about: new techniques and more self-expression. We bonded on a level that none of us expected - a level that some never knew existed. We know who we are now, alumni who will remain energetically connected through time.

This whole process started when one of the Ohio prisoners had told the other men about

<u>The Prison Coffee Table Book Project</u> we are producing. It is a book of writings and art by prisoners across America that came to fruition from an article run in a prison newsletter. The warden of GCI felt it would be beneficial for the prisoners to produce their own book and had assigned a staff sponsor to the project, which was to be sponsored by GCI's NAACP chapter. As this conversation expanded, I asked if we could fly in and hold workshops at the same time we discussed the book production. Administration said yes, we booked our flights, and the rest is history. In fact, the NAACP historian said that we actually did make history. It was the first time "outside people" had flown in on their own nickel to hold such extensive workshops.

Staff took many pictures of the smiles and tears that flashed across the weekend. We created stories of miracles about how boundaries that had dominated for decades crumbled, allowing the men to become friends where tradition and fear had stopped them before. There was a unification of spirits that continues to reshape lives and encourage seeing things, each other, and selves differently. The letters we received from the alumni speak of love, joy and creativity. They are now inspiring each other, and my heart swells from the growing experience. The plans of collaborative and collective efforts are on the drawingboard for writing, music, and drama workshops inside several prisons. There is talk that the workshops will be part of their educational course syllabi. We hope to create a public awareness of prison anthropology.

As we look back on this and try to find the golden thread of what exactly happened from May 25 through May 29, 2006, we examine the puzzle and believe that it was the fact that we looked the men in the eyes, touched them, focused on who they have become, and treated them as the individuals they are. They felt validated and cared for. They talked of one day finding love and joy, of not being a number with pre-conceived labels. They spoke of respect, intelligence, laughter, truth, and of being seen and touched. We spoke of the same things. Perhaps this process has and will continue to have a positive effect on recidivism in America.

~ The End of Four Days inside Grafton Prison

For me, there were many epiphanies and moments of enduring and endearing learning throughout those four days inside GCI because it was so far out of the range of normalcy. Everywhere I looked, everything that I did was a profound learning experience for me. It is my intention to briefly relate some of those resolving thoughts as they have developed for me.

First and foremost, prisoners are people too. People – not economic units. They come with a history and a future. Prisons are not just cement and steel structures that are filled with the most horrible murderers and rapists. Over half of the people who are caged inside prison walls are there for non-violent crimes. Ninety-five percent of the people who are incarcerated will return to a community that is not prepared to handle the challenges that come with reentry. A community that is not ready for them. Another interesting statistic was told to me by a former ODRC director: he estimated one in five prisoners to be innocent. Our justice system - just isn't. I believe the majority of people, who have not had any real connection to the justice system, think prisons are for inflicting punishment on criminals. This can often include judges and other individuals who are in authoritative positions but have not really examined the phenomenon of incarceration. In reality, punitive (inflicting punishment) is the opposite of rehabilitating. Punitive does not model positive, lasting change. And, considering most prisoners will be returning to community, isn't positive change the most desirable outcome of prison time? When the gavel goes down and the judge sentences an individual to serve time in prison, the punishment is the loss of freedom. We hear old clichés like "lock 'em up and throw away the key;" "give 'em bread and water and let 'em rot in a cell;" "I hope he is raped and beaten every day."

Why do we continue to think that we can fix the problem with the same level of thinking that created it to begin with? Idleness and the severe lack of quality programs inside prisons feed the deconstruction of human beings at their core. Considering we humans have a strong tendency to assess others through the lenses of our own class rules and experiences, it is no surprise a majority of us think humans - who are already stifled from the lack of social skills and who have grown up struggling just to struggle in an under-served, marginalized lower class neighborhood – should learn from their mistakes and be able to function on our level when they are released from prison. I have, indeed, found prisoners, for the most part, have a strong desire to participate in programs where they are treated like people, not a subhuman subculture. Many of them would pursue and earn college degrees if the means was attainable. Prisoners do not seek to be idle; they hate it. They lead a life of abnormal confinement and they are aware that they must be proactive about creating a lifestyle that guards them against their own mental and physical deterioration. Prisoners live in an information vacuum where written words are read and reread until they disintegrate.

I believe the majority of prisoners, over time, fundamentally desire to create and to serve. They seek to find their identity and value through their interactions and relationships, which is a major shift for most of them. That is what generates all of the writing, poetry, sewing, art and music inside the walls. They hyperfocus on organizational details and team work, display a high level of manners and well-thought-out consideration, and communicate on levels that I still struggle to fully comprehend. They gather their hugs from subtle words and signs in a world of extreme deprivation. A world where the most minute physical contact does not go unnoticed, and, is received as hugely positive - or hugely negative.

It is difficult for us as a society to examine the positives and negatives, especially in light of sociology theories that teach society is responsible for the construction of the self. We see support of this thought in the looking glass theory, the self-fulfilling prophecy, and the broken glass theory, just to name a few. Positivism suggests humans will often adapt and respond in equal reciprocity to their environment. My observation and experience inside prison classrooms has been if the program brings positive reinforcement and education incorporating audio, visual, and haptic paths of learning, the class retention rate will remain high. Most sober prisoners seek self-value and purpose. They are seeking information for success and social acceptance. They want to help their families and communities thrive, and to stop generational trauma.

If society creates the self, then it makes sense that society must correct her mistakes through realistic, practical, holistic education and social asset building designed to mend families, not just individuals. This would also suggest that frontline prison staff would be required to have, display, and maintain the necessary education to move from punitive to asset-building behavior and policing; that they would be able to model that which we seek. This is very rarely the case, however.

I would submit there is further breakdown of relationship building skills, social interaction skills, and emotional health from the time an individual enters prison and the date they are released back into community. They may gain book knowledge, education, vocational skills, but they have no healthy way to practice and grow their people skills. It is the reverse that happens.

When men are released back into community, they suffer from many extreme and unseen obstacles that are rarely recognized or talked about. One of the first adjustments they have to become conscious of is that as a prisoner they become self-centered in order to survive. That means the focus has to be kept on the greater good for self. Often this cognitive pattern is identified as being selfish by outside therapists, family or general citizens. It is not. Selfish means to hoard and be stingy unless it is primarily advantageous to self to do otherwise.

There is a specific set of hidden rules inside prisons that allows them to share and care for one another in a very compassionate way. Self-centered and selfish are very different traits. However, we on the outside can fail to note the differences. Sometimes this is a mere result of our projection or need to manipulate people we might struggle to identify with. However, ex-prisoners must become aware of their self-centered tendencies and strive to reframe their position within community outside the walls.

Due to forced, regimented structure, prisoners lose the ability to plan. It is not unlike the populations of Russia right after the USSR fell. The people had been so controlled by the government they had lost the concept of planning. A missionary that had gone to Russia to help the churches stabilize and the communities rebuild told me that the biggest challenge he battled was that the people couldn't comprehend planning a church calendar for a year out. Hard to believe, isn't it? Prisoners are impaired by the same suppression. Yet, when they are released, they are given an excessive amount of reporting, classes, community service, job hunting, house hunting, transportation, phone service, shopping, meal planning, clothing preparation, and much more of what we outsiders do routinely. Even the act of having a calendar to write it down, and then planning to look at the calendar as a guide, is a very big challenge for most ex-prisoners. And, they can get a technical violation for missing appointments and be sent back to prison. Try to imagine being so frozen in place and in such complete overload – we can't unless we've been there. People in authority over these individuals often think that the ex-prisoner is failing out of rebellion or laziness. This is a big challenge for reentry.

Another predictable obstacle is that prisoners lose their ability to believe in happy endings. Common scenarios such as the following one can certainly reinforce that and create the attitude that one is better off not even to expect happiness. A prisoner saved a Snickers candy bar for three months so he would have something special for his birthday. The morning of his birthday, a couple of block guards found out. For amusement they strip searched him; took photos of his butt-naked body to chart his tattoos, of which he had none, and took the candy bar. They then shook down his cell and personal belongings, leaving it scattered all over the floor. One of the guards opened the Snickers on his way out of the cell, and as he bit into it, he wished the prisoner a happy birthday. Guards with idle hands and minds also model behavior.

Is it any wonder that prisoners lose their belief in happy endings? My observations continue to be that most prisoners have undergone so much loss as a child that they grew to expect the worst, even before they entered prison. Prison serves to fuel the disbelief. They have adapted to handling loss better than gain. Often they will actually create the loss because it is more familiar. It is easy to see these patterns reflected in the lack of motivation to plan activities or celebrations even after they are freed back into community.

A prisoner's perception of life in general changes dramatically within the first year of incarceration and this change has a strong bearing on his relationships. I refer to it as prison gerontology. I would argue that when you take away a man's clothes, car, jewelry, women, family, house, and other material belongings through which he identifies himself within his social circles, then he has to go inside himself to discover who he is outside of his property and people or he will effectively lose his mind. Prison takes away mirrors or reflections of self; photos to document one's life; and intimate relationships where someone else bears witness to an individual's life. I would submit that when we humans lose our literal reflection, we often misplace our identity and are catapulted into the need for recapturing it based on other criteria.

Prison life plunges men into their middle age crisis years before the natural cycle. I define middle age crisis as the period of time in which one's physical attributes change significantly and the individual begins to focus on inner spiritual accomplishments, or ontological quests. It's an awakening that life is not all about sex. There's a spiritual element - and they may feel like a spiritual embryo in a state of panic. This usually kicks in around age forty. In prison, the absence of stuff, relationships, and reflections has the power to heighten the sense of aging. In fact, most prisoners tell me that they feel like they are twice their age.

This can cause mental chaos upon reentry, especially since they have not had healthy opportunities to mature in intimate, emotional relationships beyond the initial point of incarceration – yet they may have grown far beyond their years in many other areas of their mental, intellectual, and spiritual being. In other words, if a man becomes incarcerated at the age of eighteen and is released twenty years later, he will likely have digressed emotionally and will be drawn to girls who are 18 or younger, yet his view of everything else will likely be that of a sixty year old man; because he has lived in a grim environment for 20 years. They are caught between their lost youth and their gained wisdom, and the outside world has no way to be aware of their dilemma – even prisoners probably don't understand it.

Also, upon release, prisoners have lost their ability to trust almost anything or anyone. Along with that, they also lose their ability to relax and accept human touch and affection. They have gained the bitter knowledge that nothing is too extreme for one human to do to another, whether they are peers or the person who is in charge of their safety. As a result, the creative mind runs wild sorting out limitless possibilities, plausibility, and probabilities on a negative scale that we civilians can never imagine nor connect with. And, if the prisoner has been abused as a child, his imagination already reads like a horror movie, which may be reflected in his crimes. This cognitive patterning can have a severe impact on all relationships, and most assuredly on intimate ones, even after a prisoner manages to rehabilitate himself.

Prison also creates a massive amount of vicarious trauma. In 2010, a man who was incarcerated for thirty years for the rape of a child was exonerated and freed on DNA evidence. He asked if I could guide him as he walked back into the outside world as an international celebrity. He won the crown for the human who had served the most time prior to being exonerated by DNA evidence. What a trophy.

After the cameras and crowds subsided and we were finally able to just talk privately, he said to me, "I want to tell you something. You know I've been in prison for 30 years, and I know all the things that people and movies say about prisoners. I want to assure you that I didn't do any of that stuff. But, even though I didn't do any of it, I heard it, saw it, and smelled it 24x7 and I feel dirty. I have to figure out how to get clean. Do you understand? It messed me up."

I have watched him for nearly three years. His exoneration made him a very wealthy man. But, his lack of trust has kept him from seeking professional help, and I understand that. Thirty years of suppressing emotions and having been toyed with by staff continue to imprison him. It took him two years to begin to plan his life and to travel. He even bought his house within an hour's drive of the prison he called home for over ten years. He still prefers to not be alone. However, it isn't difficult for me to see the anguish that Post Traumatic Stress Disorder has spinning inside his head. The possibilities, plausibility, and probabilities never leave, as I understand them. There are no happy endings, remember? He has lost his glow of freedom and has isolated himself more than I would like to see. He continues to stage and act out his pain with those closest to him, because somehow that works best for these men who have lost the ability to show emotions.

The federal public defender once asked me how many of the ex-prisoners I thought were able to return to being normal in their emotional response and day to day rationale. My answer was zero. I used this metaphor to describe what I have observed. A man who has never been jailed is thinking about cheating on his wife. He ponders what his wife might do if he does cheat, and he concludes that there are four basic scenarios that might happen: 1) she will never know, 2) she will find out and leave him forever, 3) she will find out and forgive him, 4) she will find out, they will separate, and then they will get back together. There will likely be a lot of loud language if she finds out, and maybe some physical outbursts, but probably nothing life-threatening. I realize that I am simplifying this, but you get the picture, right? Now, let's take a man who has done time inside prison and put him in the same situation. His scenarios of what might happen would go more like this: 1) she will find out and will kill me in my sleep, 2) she will cut off my penis while I'm asleep, 3) she will pour boiling grits on my groins while I'm asleep, 4) she will do something to send me back to prison.

One of the gifts of prison is a new and expanded version of emotional buttons and thought processes. They are limitless in all their facets and they won't ever go away. The difficult part of this is that the people who have never been incarcerated are not even aware the shift happened or the thoughts are going on. They don't even know what they are dealing with. And, the above scenario also has a flip side. When things fall out of the ordinary pattern of behavior, an ex-prisoner is quick to jump to negative conclusions. Their minds will justify the possibilities and not likely look at any scenario other than from a loss vantage point. Then they go into fear and anger and begin acting out before they have any true answers. This is why open communication is so vital for these relationships to be able to survive. It applies beyond intimate relationships. People dealing with the ex-prisoner really do have to rise above their personal feelings and ask enough questions to get clues as to what is playing out in the ex-prisoner's mind, in order to bring them into reality and its impact on people around them. That's not the normal way of handling personal conflict.

So, who out here has the knowledge and

experience to guide these people through the dark night of the soul? How do we fix or even adjust all of this damage so people can live happy, successful lives back inside community. This question haunts me without cessation.

Chapter Two
RELOCATION TO OHIO

When I had returned to New Mexico from the GCI trip, my nephew, Clint, who lived in Youngstown, Ohio, suggested I move to Ohio to invest in the cheap real estate market. The more I looked at Realtor.com, the more pencils I burned through. It wasn't too long before I calculated how much my sprawling New Mexico ranch casa would earn on the market, and how many Ohio houses I could buy with the equity. There were literally hundreds of century-old houses listed between $5-15k.

Being fully engaged in social and prison reform by this point and recognizing that my lack of mastery of the Spanish language would be too much of a handicap for me to continue working within the New Mexico prisons, I listened to Clint. We began to put the pencil to the numbers and brainstorm the possibilities of accumulating real estate, paying ex-prisoners to rehab the houses, and then providing housing as part of our reentry program. The plan also allowed us to generate revenue streams for the many reentry programs we had begun to pull together, including the community garden and culinary program he, an executive chef, would direct.

In addition, the three hundred fifty national prisoners that I regularly corresponded with had been adamant that if I was going to serve the prison population, then I needed to live among their families in order to gain a better understanding of the challenges and cultures. That made good sense to me. I was already reeled into the service and I needed to be where I could make the most impact. That would be an oppressed, minority community. And, Ohio made sense to the extremist in me, especially since the state is deemed by the department of justice to be the most progressive in the arena of rehabilitation and reentry. Many things led me to the little city of Canton, about sixty-five miles south of Cleveland, and it has worked as a central location for my extensive travel.

We left the New Mexico desert the first of December and moved into Canton, a small town buried in snow. As spring slowly unfolded and the winter began to melt away, the people emerged from their houses like bears from hibernation. I was more curious than the many neighborhood cats. My front porch became my classroom, and I took a front row seat. I was so taken by my observations and our experiences that I wrote the following anthropologic paper. I have elected to include it in this writing for foundation. It is critical to present insight into the culture that dominated childhood development and is the basis for the deeply rooted a priori beliefs of the majority of prisoners. It is important, I believe, to be reminded often of the distinct differences between classes and cultures in order to design effective and progressive social asset building programs and opportunities to reverse negative generational life cycles.

The Front Porch Society

My rearing began in 1947 and took place in the panhandle of Texas, where everything seems to spread out. The landscape is so flat that lights from feed lots, some 35 miles away, can be seen from the 27th floor of downtown buildings. As a result I grew up accustomed to having my own living space.

Beyond the very early years of my youth, I don't recall who my neighbors were unless our lives overlapped in some out of the ordinary event. Even then, the acquaintance seemed to always be transitional. Kids played with kids from school or church. We rode bikes on the school parking lot, skated on the sidewalks, and built forts in the vacant lots. Other than one snapshot memory of running, playing and giggling on a porch that seemed to wrap around the house, I have no recollection of big country porches on any of the many houses we occupied during my childhood, or even teen years. I remember small concrete-step porches being functional as a means of entering and exiting a house: the gateway into the guarded and territorial lives of neighbors.

I grew up trained to keep my family life private and not shared with the families who lived around my house. I was never aware of any neighborhood support systems and the word community was another word for county. Even the wintry act of getting a car jump-started would usually entail calling a professional mechanic in lieu of bothering a neighbor. Though borrowing a cup of sugar or an egg was still tolerated, it came with its own label of need, so it was frowned upon and discouraged. Not having transportation to the grocery store or hospital meant walking, bussing, or paying a taxi. Infringing on a neighbor to this degree was just not done in my lower-middle-class neighborhood. In fact, it was debated whether a family member would be phoned and infringed upon for individual or personal needs.

The preceding may seem harsh to those who have experienced the northern hundred-year-old neighborhoods where garages are not standard, but big sprawling front porches are. Multi-storied houses are built within spitting range of each other, with lawns so small that mowing can almost be accomplished with a pair of kitchen scissors. Wooden homes that have sheltered families for over a century, built so close together the un-insulated walls carry the neighboring conversations, broadcasting them to nearby ears.

So, the story began in December, 2006, when I sold my rambling New Mexico ranch home, packed up my two granddaughters and moved to Canton, Ohio. My plan was to move to an older, impoverished neighborhood, otherwise known as *The Hood*, where I could buy, renovate, and rent about a dozen homes, in order to build up the financial nest egg that would help to support our non-profit organization that actively strives to make a difference in the lives of America's prisoners and their families.

After many conversations with local authority figures, I picked out a house for my girls and myself to move into. It appeared to be in an area of *The Hood* where the city was concentrating efforts to "turn around" the negative forces of prostitution, gangs, and drugs. Just four houses down from ours was

a four million dollar elementary school in its
first year of use. The school principal had a
doctorate in special education and was
very present and active in his school district
as a whole, and in the lives of his individual
students. Behind the school, the city had
recently demolished fourteen blighted
century-old houses and sold the reallocated
lots to contractors who had agreed to build
new, singlefamily replacement homes. The
lots were divided to have more acreage,
and the house specifications required the
houses to be multi-storied with a garage for
off-street parking. And, they must have a
large front porch. In addition, a new police
substation had been located four blocks
away, and a federal Weed and Seed grant
had been awarded to the area. The signs
seemed to support my choice of location.

Ours was a big, boxy, two-story white house
with a newly rebuilt porch spanning across
its front. Since we were located on a corner,
we had the prestige of more "breathing" and
"viewing" room. And as the winter began to
melt, and people began to venture outside
of their homes like ground hogs awakening
from hibernation, they began to assess the
exterior of their living spaces: picking up
trash that had been buried under months of
snow; checking out shrubbery; sweeping off
porches; noticing who had moved in or out
since winter blanketed the neighborhood.
Unaware that we, too, were part of this

awakening, the girls and I quickly recognized that the steps of our front porch naturally made good seats from which to observe our new neighborhood; not realizing that it would be the neighbors, not the layout of the neighborhood, that would envelope our lives. At the same time, unbeknownst to us, many of the people were wondering why on earth a white grandmother would move her family from the New Mexico desert to *The Hood*. Many of them had never traveled outside of the city. Most didn't know the difference between New Mexico and Old Mexico. Did we have a green card? It turned out that they had as many questions for us as we had for them. But their first question was that of trust: why were we really there and what did we want from them?

Innocent to the depth of our surroundings, the three of us set about settling in and planning for the spring. We'd need some porch furniture and a grill. Our porch was plenty big for that and it just felt good to sit outside. Lots of grass and trees and wildlife to observe. Of course, at that point, we didn't realize the extent of wildlife in *The Hood*.

Back in December, we had arrived with U-haul's longest truck, towing our 1993 Mercury station wagon, and a super-cab Ford pulling a 5x8 U-Haul trailer, all filled to capacity with our stuff. A crew of local teens showed up for unloading. In my world, this is not an uncommon move-in strategy. I look back on that fanfare and think about all the conversations that must have gone on around our arrival. Since the weather had let up a bit on that winter's day, we had, in effect, met a few neighbors as we moved in. So, as the sunshine appeared, these same individuals came over to check on us. I'd be out on the porch sipping morning coffee, and neighbors would meander over and converse with me, always seeking the answer to why we were "there."

We knew more of our neighbors the first month into spring than I had ever known in any neighborhood I'd lived in. There were kids galore on bikes, skateboards, and just playing in the street or on the school parking lot. They seemed to be everywhere, and very verbal and busy about life. Inquisitive. They were curious about us and not shy about engaging in conversation with us.

It wasn't long before the man two doors down had aired up the girls' bike tires and they were circling the blocks with a half dozen or more other kids. All were excited and on adventures of the day. Spring had arrived, and with it the neighborhood that slept quietly beneath the snow had emerged into a bustle of activity and noise, the sound of which would often not subside until the wee hours of the next morning.

As the season heated up, it became obvious that the discomfort of the sultry heat and our need to sleep at night far outweighed any consideration of crime against us. We opened all the windows and the cross-breezes blowing through the large, over-sized wooden windows cooled us. Because the house was old wood, it had its own vocabulary when anyone, including the cat, would walk in it. So, leaving lower level windows open at night was left to the security of two tiny Chihuahuas and one fair-sized coyote-sheltie named Sophie. Our windows remained open until autumn chills led us to close them.

To our advantage was the fact most occupants of *The Hood* fear dogs of any size. I did not realize at first the theft of guns or drugs would be the only motivation to break into a house in *The Hood*, and it was easy to know we had neither. We were never in any peril and felt that early on. I should add if it was known that I moved in with 250 bottles of my homemade wine, I probably would have had my basement broken into.

One of the first meaningful exchanges with neighboring kids was around 7:30 one Sunday morning when I stepped out onto the front porch with two dozen petunia seedlings in a cardboard flat in one hand, and a cup of coffee in the other. I set the flowers and the coffee down on the steps and returned to the house to get a big spoon to dig the holes for planting. I had not seen one other person outside and was actually looking forward to playing in the dirt by myself. My girls were in the house arguing over TV.

I'd hand-picked the petunias in three colors so I could make a nice design in the small six foot by two foot plot by the steps. No sooner had I turned my back to the street, bent over, and began to scoop out the dirt for the first hole, than a preschool child I'd never before seen popped up beside me and asked what I was doing. I jumped and replied, "I'm planting these pretty petunias in this little flower bed so when I sit on my porch step I can enjoy them." The child asked if she could help, and I, of course, said sure.

I went back into the house to retrieve another spoon for digging. When I returned, there were three other young children, none of which had I ever seen. Could they help too? I quickly determined the plot wouldn't hold our five bodies at one time, so I would organize us into shifts and I would be the instructor of how to plant this plot exactly as I saw it in my mind. I stuck a tree twig in the ground to mark the spots where a plant would be. I explained which colors would go where, and told the first two kids to dig their holes. I signaled to the others to get quiet and wait their turns.

As we sat on the steps watching the spoons, I came to realize these kids didn't know how to dig in the dirt. They were scraping the soil, but not digging. Kids didn't know how to play in the dirt! I felt it throughout my body. And, since I was the only one stepping up to correct the action, I knew none of the others watching saw it as problematic. I had to teach all four of them how to dig a hole in the dirt with a spoon. Following that lesson was the explanation of how fragile the life of the little plant was, and how the roots had to be securely planted in a deep hole, and gently watered in order to survive.

I'm not sure how to really describe to you the frenzy that soon developed, or the order of human spirit that drove it, but it became very clear to me that the call of the dirt to these children of *The Hood* was so compelling that they were fighting to be in the dirt and holding the plants with the utmost gentleness at the same time. My plan to control where each plant would be was soon cast aside in lieu of just letting the kids experience the process and hoping the plants would all survive at the same time.

After all were planted, the children, seeking to draw out the experience, quickly focused on the water faucet nearby. A cup at a time, they carried water and fed their plants, until the spot was flooded and I noted it was enough. We all sat tightly on the porch steps

41

and admired nature. Smiling. Accomplished.
I knew right then, to the depths of my soul,
just how important community gardens are.
I'd spoken many times of how healing dirt is
to people who have not had enough
nurturing, but this was a front-row seat. I also
realized flowers are a luxury in *The Hood*.

For weeks, these kids would bring friends by
to check on the plants and, perhaps, carry
a cup or two of water to them. I never
attached a hose to the faucet, but left the
watering to the collective cups of water. As
a result, my sitting on the steps to drink a cup
of coffee always generated new friends. I
guess the gathering of kids around my steps
brought the curiosity of the adults. It must
have at least created the feeling of safety.
Maybe the air of nurturing. I can only
speculate. But, it wasn't long before adults
were coming and introducing themselves
to me, or greeting me by name as they
passed. It intrigued me.

There were always a lot of people walking by.
Walking because they had no other means
to travel, or because they were only going
within the borders of the four-square-block
neighborhood, or they were transacting
various business deals that were better left to
foot traffic. Hence, I began to examine the
tradition of walking right down the middle of
the street as opposed to walking on the
sidewalks. Where I came from, streets are

for cars. Sidewalks are for people. Walking in the street can get you run over. Here, in *The Hood*, rarely did people use sidewalks. Cars and people jointly choreographed the movement on the asphalt. Why?

So, I studied the physicality of the sidewalks. They were narrow, uneven and broken with tree roots and decades of use. The law is that the property owners are responsible for the condition of the sidewalks, so the roots of the huge maple trees break the squares, the snow and salt decay the concrete, and just like most everything else in *The Hood*, no effort is made to fix it. So, walking on the sidewalks would mean walking while looking down to keep from stumbling.

Then I studied the people walking by. The sidewalks were within ten feet of the porch steps of homes. This was *The Hood*. Territorial. Things happen in *The Hood* that can cost you your life if you are not vigilant and quick to react. Walking on the sidewalk would mean looking down instead of up and around your vicinity. In addition, it would put you very close to any activity the occupants in the houses might produce. Neighbors might be in a state of mind to perceive that you were "in their stuff" and that could draw a bullet.

I don't think that the tradition of walking down the center of the street is done for mere exhibition, as many white people had told me. I believe it is rooted in survival. That conclusion can be drawn before examining the additional fact that few people walk by themselves, and walking single-file on narrow, broken sidewalks does not allow for the exchange of conversation.

Late one night, early on in the spring, I was sitting on the front porch drinking a glass of wine, hoping to see the raccoon appear from the gutter drain and climb up to the top balcony of the neighboring duplex, in yet another attempt to go through the window and get food. From the darkened porch across the street and down one came a deep male voice greeting me and laughing. With beer in hand, he walked out of the shadow and into view, and on over to welcome me to *The Hood*. I offered him a step and we laughed and watched the nocturnal animals appear. A man of the night, he knew right where to look to see raccoons, opossums, bats, and an occasional skunk. That man, Don, became a good friend. It helped that he was alcoholic and I had homemade wine stacked in my basement. Before long we were making ten o'clock the hour to show up with glass in hand, a cork screw, a bottle of wine to share, and one for Don to carry home afterwards. We trusted each other and so our exchange became more insightful. He'd manage his many cell phone calls, at the same time pointing out to me the various activities going on around me. A white man half my age, he delighted in my naivety about *The Hood*, while at the same time casting a safety net around me and mine. Soon, our laughter and wine glasses became an attraction for others to join us, all guarding the source of free alcohol and safe conversation. No one, however, came up to me or my house until someone, usually Don, told them it was safe and I could be trusted. He always told them of my work on behalf of prisoners. Sometimes we had three-bottle nights, but I rarely got through two glasses of wine myself.

I don't remember ever laughing as much or as deeply as I did that summer on the porch in *The Hood*. I was more than willing to exchange wine for the stories of life and times from passing prostitutes. The raw sincerity of the tellers never failed to amaze me. Conversations about every phase of life would be intertwined and personal information that I would have never shared was right out there reverberating off of the aged walls and being laughed at by the victims. Lack and illness. Crime and punishment.

What was even more foreign to me was that the people who lacked the most were willing to share what little they had. Though transitional in its nature, there was real community surrounding my porch. More than once I retrieved a bowl of stew or a sandwich from my kitchen. In fact, it became a way of meal planning. It became an honor to be able to provide a meal on the porch, or to drive someone to an appointment or the grocery store the next morning. Having a station wagon was good.

I remember Don coming over and telling me about a prostitute who had gotten badly beaten up and he had her upstairs recovering in his apartment. He wouldn't get his back pain killer prescription filled before the next day and he had nothing strong enough to cut her pain.

She wasn't eating. He was known to be the haven for tired, hurt, hungry hookers and underwent a lot of neighborhood criticism for his taking them in. I called him Father Teresa, which always made him laugh and say it must be true because he was living the life of a "None." I asked to meet the girl and was led up the dark stairs to the tiny room where she lay. I'd never been inside Don's building, yet it was no different than I had envisioned it.

There on a small bed was a middle-aged black woman, curled up in need. Don softly touched her and introduced us. She was startled and unsure. I told her who I was and asked her when she had last eaten.

Three days ago. She heard my accent and commented that her people were from the South. I asked if she liked hominy and pork, and she perked up and told me about her grandmother cooking it for her. I described a New Mexican dish called posole and she promised to eat if I would cook it for her. And she did. In fact, the entire duplex ate from that big pot. They all needed nurturing. I felt honored to have been invited into that room as a trusted part of community.

When we first arrived in Ohio, one of the main goals listed on my eleven year old's Individual Education Plan was to learn to socialize, attract and retain friends. She had been in exclusive special education classes since age three and this was the first year for her to be in main stream. Because abnormal behavior is the norm for special education classes, Britt had come up deficient and very frustrated that she didn't have a bunch of friends like her older sister, Falicia; not even one friend. This had become critical to her development and well-being. Rarely did she feel included on the playground, and rarely did she have a friend over to our house in New Mexico. So, when the children of *The Hood* mounted their bikes and asked her to come along, she was in heaven. Pure heaven!

The first couple of months, however, Britt, my younger granddaughter who is very literal and doesn't comprehend humor or sarcasm, was repeating things she shouldn't and being confrontational in ways that would have gotten her banned or hurt if she hadn't had her older sister to mediate. It was a long and stressful process, but never was there a day that we didn't have groups of children coming and going from our porch.

The unspoken rule of *The Hood* was that kids stay on the porch and don't go inside anyone's house where they might be out of sight and in harm's way, or accused of theft. My personal rule was that my girls were never to be alone. Never. I had to know where they were and where their friends lived. I wanted to look in the boys' eyes, asked them where they lived, and call them by name. The neighborhood girls were more talkative and transparent. It wasn't too long before my rules were known and respected and no one would let my girls walk alone. I would try to keep other girls from walking alone, but they didn't see the danger nor were they used to the concern. I worried about them.

The summer of 2007 was the summer both my girls will refer to when they talk of childhood memories. Britt learned to have friends and be part of the group. She learned to be aware of her environment and the laws of cause and effect. Falicia learned change can be fun and life has many dimensions. I learned to sit on the porch and listen.

I remember one hot night last summer, nearly every family stayed outside on the porch in search of any breeze. I finally went upstairs and crawled into bed, with all windows wide open. About four houses down the street, a party had been going on for several hours. It was now early morning and I became aware that no fights had arisen from the drinking and drugs. The group had continued to grow with the night, and now there were men who were singing and laughing. I could not see them from my bedroom window, but I knew the house. It was a century-old stone home that had been converted to a fourplex. It had a tall cement porch with columns across the front of it and this porch had morphed into a stage on this evening.

Men began to recite poetry that spoke of prison, of hardships, of being black in America. For hours, even until the sun came up, these many men sang, delivered poetry, chanted lyrics of oppression, and played virtual prison instruments using rhythmic slapping of their bodies and vocal percussion sounds to perform lengthy improv concerts. As the performance became freer and more uninhibited, spanning beyond the now and into the annals of history, I realized that most all of these men were playing from the heart and soul of the lament of their prison time. Dark night of the soul times. I felt so insufficient that I had no way to record or film this phenomenon that rang throughout *The Hood* that night. That one night last summer. No one fought. The melodic laughter of deep-voiced men was a gift to all who listened.

It was quite common to hear black women laughing, talking, cursing, and yelling in *The Hood*, any time of day or night. But, that night, I remember thinking I had no recall of hearing the laughter of grown men echoing through *The Hood* before then. The men were generally soft spoken and quiet unless under the influence of the bottle, in which case their loudness did not take on the form of laughter. Even those occasions were rare. It would have made such an extraordinary documentary. Such a window into the depth of manhood. They all came together with the muses and they let us watch and hear. It shall never leave me, yet I have no way to play it or recreate it for anyone absent that summer's night in *The Hood*.

When we packed up and left New Mexico headed north to Ohio, my granddaughter Falicia was fourteen and in her last year of middle school. She had left a preppy school and valley girl conversations. She was maturing into a woman and had no concept of how serious life could be. Life was a facade without struggle. We'd been in

New Mexico where Latinos were the majority, and now we were in *The Hood* where African-Americans were the majority, and Latinos weren't from Mexico. Anyone who was actually Hispanic or Latino in Ohio came with a lot of negative stigma. Being very upset with the up-rooting, Falicia was not all smiles nor did she know how to respond to her new surroundings. The fact that she is Irish and Comanche Indian with green eyes, dark auburn hair to her waist, and the beauty of a tall top-model was proving itself to be as much a liability as an asset in her new school. The kids thought she was a Goth from Mexico. She kept her mouth closed and her arms crossed. The fact that the males all began asking her out the first day, and surrounding her in attempts to engage in conversation, turned out to be a good thing. She chose the quarter-back and for the next seven months he guarded her and educated her in the life of *The Hood*. Under his tough-guy attitude was an abusive family life that created a callous that covered up the naivety of who he really was. But, as long as she was his girl, no one messed with her.

Now, one year later, she appears to be the most popular girl in high school. She is greatly loved, respected, and guarded by all; and is no one's girlfriend per se. She has embraced the role of counselor and offers the safe haven of our home to other teens who just need breathing room or rest.

A good meal, washed clothes and a safe
night's sleep can easily make the difference
in whether a teen drops out of school or not.
Whether he gives up or not.

Prior to our Ohio experience, I had always
wondered why black people seemed to
always know all about each other's family
members and lives. Now I know. It's called
community. In this Hood, I was able to lie
in bed with windows open and listen to the
various scenarios of family playing-out on the
porches, in the streets, or inside houses with
opened windows. My ears would move from
one house to the other. I knew about the
lives of families I'd never actually met. I knew
names, habits, jobs, finances, etc. On many
occasions I lay there thinking how quickly
I would have dialed 911 in the past, but
realizing now most things don't merit putting
people in prison, nor further tearing families
apart by trying to intervene in situations that
would work themselves out on their own
stages. Unless a life or child is in danger, let
humanity work it out in the context of their
own community.

After Don moved to Michigan, the gangs
moved into our block just as he said they
would. We moved out of *The Hood* and
into Church Row almost a year to the day
that we had moved into it. We are still in
walking distance, but we are definitely not
in *The Hood*. We have nuns and churches

for neighbors. We still live on a corner. Our house is a big beautiful brick English Tudor surrounded by huge hovering pine trees. Though we live at a major intersection of four lane traffic, we seldom can hear the "outside" through our insulated, brick walls. We watch it through the lens of a ten foot picture window facing the neighborhood we left behind. Each of us still strains to identify characteristics of the many people who come walking down the long road between there and here and secretly hope they are old friends walking to see us, as often they are. They bring us tales of neighboring kids still congregating on the porch of the vacant house we once occupied. I hear them tell my kids they miss us, and my kids sincerely tell them how much they miss the old neighborhood. I know this void will increase as summer unfolds here.

With all the comfort, quiet, and safety of this home, my kids long to be back on the porch where the bustle is. Where life is transparent and real. Where tears and laughter are given equal time. Where survival replaces judgment. Where a village is struggling with raising children. Where noise is normal.

We seem to have everything here but a porch. We have a huge, landscaped front lawn, a three-car garage with an automatic opener and a large loft, nearly three times the living space, a garden spot, a large cement backyard patio hidden by huge pine trees where many summer barbeques will be staged, a fireplace, and a laundry chute. But no front porch.

However we choose to frame it, it appears to me we human beings seem to function better as a whole when we have a neutral stage built into our society upon which the child in each of us can reach out and interact with one another in such a way as to bond through interactions that nurture us and compassionately carry us through our daily lives. Simply stated, perhaps it is in fact community that we all ultimately and foremost seek out, and something as simple as the latent function of sprawling front porches can fulfill that social need.

~~ The End of The Front Porch Society

As I progressed through the seasons that year, my revelation was that these anthropological behaviors had evolved out of survival choices, not rebellion against whites or middle class. We tend to get caught up in assumptions, and thus judgments, about people, both as a group and individual, inside and outside our own social class. This is usually a reflection of lack of information on the viewer's part. But, the fact is a social group of people doesn't just wake up one morning and, out of the blue, declare their customs and beliefs, not even in a state of rebellion.

History carves out the distinctions of cultures and subcultures. They are based on the struggles, events, resources, and environment of the group over generations of time. It is important to realize that even ethnological studies deal with only the most apparent information as viewed from the perspective of an outsider. In my opinion, a true ethnological study would have to be done by a person who grew up in the subculture; obtained a high level of education that would allow them to thrive in an upper class, and then to review the culture they grew up in. And even then, there would be a *priori* beliefs that would probably not surface, but would effect the study.

I consider it a privilege to have the opportunity to work so closely with the prisoners. But still, after over seven years of being accepted inside prisoner circles, I am very aware I will never be a young, black male from inner Cleveland. My best work comes from listening to those people tell their truth of the intimate details of their lives and in hearing their opinion of what is broken and what might have a positive effect on their people. If I can live in the midst of a culture while I have the opportunity to listen and observe as one of them, then it is as ideal as I know how to make it. That is why I decided to include The Front Porch Society as a vantage point in hopes some of my epiphanies and perceptions might influence programming, or at least help to explain some of my curriculum choices.

I think of how a place that I would have never considered going into until I did gave me such great fulfillment, such rich experiences that summer. I must, however, admit that my increased knowledge over the years causes me to seldom drive through that part of town. I have learned enough to have some fear. Especially as an outsider.

Now, as I reread my journal on living in *The Hood*, I realize there are many cultural insights hidden between the lines, ones I don't wish to assume the reader grasps. They are too important to be missed, as we study how society as a whole can help carve plausible paths out of impoverished imprisonment. Therefore I shall expand on those points, for clarity.

Let's begin with assumptions about how children sleep. Personally, I've always had my own bedroom. My girls expect to have their own spaces. Middle class rules allow for children to have their own bedrooms. But this is not at all the norm for poverty. There was a house cattycornered from ours in *The Hood* where a black family comprised of fourteen children, two women, and one man lived. The children were often at our house and I found their company to be most enjoyable. After about a month, the four younger girls received permission from their mom to come inside to play. They were quick to run up and down the stairs to look at everything. When they realized that all three of us had our own bedrooms, they were quite taken back. They couldn't believe the possibility. One of them was sitting on Falicia's bed, pensively rocking back and forth. She broke her silence to say, "When I grow up, I'm going to have a bed. I've never slept on a bed before."

I remember making an effort to conceal my shock as I asked her where she slept now. She went on to explain most of the children slept in the attic. They each had their own pillow and blanket. "It's really cold up there when it snows," she told me. Her attention then went to Falicia's closet of clothes and the jewelry box which sat atop her mirrored dresser. She explained without my asking that she didn't have drawers either. I stood there thinking about how hot those old attics get on the scorching summer's nights, nothing between the floor and beating sun except old dusty wood and black tar shingles – and a dozen children, in this case. I learned that their story wasn't so rare as I'd wanted to believe.

The three times I stood on their front porch, gathering children, the man was at the stove cooking. My girls had been inside the house and told stories of how the roaches were so thick they were running up and down the walls and they feared they would fall into the food. Roaches are considered as common as are the mice, bats, and raccoons. To be clear, my cat caught our mouse and I subscribed to Terminix – a luxury.

In poverty, neighbors are resources. People are the only tangible resource. The more you are connected, the easier survival becomes. An example: if you knew me, on Wednesday evenings you could ride a couple of miles to the Total Living Center in my station wagon, attend a service, and bring home a couple of boxes filled with free food. My car was also used for doctor or hospital trips if the patient was too ill to walk or take the bus. However, the trust element doesn't change. And the children still abide by two major rules: be home when the street lights go off, and do not go inside any house other than your own unless your mom knows the people and has checked it out first. Danger lurks in the dark and when other people can't see you.

I never took my car for granted. I panic to think about even a day without a good car. However, walking is the main mode of transportation in poverty. Second would be public transportation. And third would be to own a bike, which would likely be stolen shortly after you acquired it. Bikes are stolen and re-stolen to the point it looks more like community sharing. Hence, bikes are just required to work, not to be pretty or personalized. Cars are indeed a real luxury in an impoverished culture. However, without a valid driver's license and active car insurance, the driver can end up in a criminal court with penalties. Cars also require expensive gasoline, and since people are expected to share resources, the owner of the car ends up feeding the gas tank more often than not. Thus, it is not a surprise that many in poverty have not traveled outside their city.

Somewhat related is the lawn mower. If a person got lucky enough to own a lawn mower, and could keep it from being stolen, they could actually start a mowing business that could at least feed them. But this is not the norm. There aren't garages, or chains and locks. Those are luxury items. Hence, I found when my grass was in need of mowing, several people would end up knocking on my door, offering to mow my grass with my mower for ten dollars. Sometimes I let them. They call this their landscaping business.

One of the routine pleasures the neighborhood children looked forward to was riding the Salvation Army bus to Sunday School and church every Sunday morning.

Like clockwork, the rugged old bus would round the corner and the children, who had gotten themselves up and ready on time, would climb aboard with great excitement. The Salvation Army would praise them, feed them, teach them songs, and tell them about God's unconditional love. It was a neighborhood ritual. The parents loved this also, because for half a day on Sundays their children were gone and attended to. As a sidebar, the children most generally were also responsible for getting themselves up and ready for school during the week. Speaking of schools, remember reading about the new school that was just four doors down from our house? Well, by the third year, it was converted to a charter school which focuses on the arts. It is a prestigious school. A child has to undergo interviews and auditions in order to attend. I had asked Tom, the principal, why they picked this school to convert. It didn't make sense that the neighborhood children would be asked to commute outside of their district every day. They were already on their own, for the most part. He said the committee picked the school that had the most transient population so it would have the least effect on stationary families. Oh, and new houses the city built next door to the new school: it took two years to get buyers for the $120k houses.

Back in December, when we first pulled our

U-Haul caravan up to the curb of that corner house, there were four young men who came around to meet us. I hired them to unload us. They worked very hard and diligently for three days, unloading to three floors, and assembling and rearranging heavy furniture. I was so thankful for them. Afterwards, I handed them each a one hundred dollar bill, and felt it wasn't nearly enough for the work they'd done. But, to them, it seemed like a thousand. One sixteen year old cried. He said he needed clothes and new shoes. That was one of my first key insights. A latent benefit of hiring the locals to unload us was I offered trust to them; they saw all we owned, and they would have taken it personally had we ever been the target of a break-in. At the time, I was simply glad to have strong bodies available to help us move in.

Obviously we moved a whole lot of stuff from New Mexico to our new home in Ohio. So, it should be easy to understand why I was so puzzled and dismayed that, when poor people move out of a house, they leave most of their belongings for the landlord to throw out to the curb for trash pickup. It made no sense to me. I'd see televisions, kitchen appliances, baby clothes and toys. Just big heaps of personal belongings that I knew the tenants wouldn't have the money to replace. I called it stupid and lazy. I blamed it on drug-altered minds, or overbearing men. My neighbor, Don, waited until the end of my midnight rant about a mother of two babies leaving all her stuff before he replied "How would she have moved all of it? They don't have a car, nor do they know anyone who has a car who would be willing to move it every time the rent is due. Hell, she didn't even have a way to go get boxes to pack in. When they leave, they take only what they can carry on the day they get evicted." I sat there owning the blinders of my middle class rant. I must also say I never was aware of other neighbors rummaging through the abandoned heaps. Maybe it was because they knew it would just be more for them to eventually leave behind, or that they didn't want to appear to have less than an evicted neighbor. We can only speculate.

This nomad lifestyle does not teach children and future adults the skill of taking care of toys or belongings so they will last a long time and look new. The curiosity or immediate gratification that comes from taking them apart, or the coping skill of venting anger through destruction, becomes more appealing when a child considers ownership to be temporal. And, if one can't comprehend attending to one's own belongings in the name of longevity and asset building, how could we expect them to comprehend attending to the property of others, such as the house they live in?

Landlords quickly learn that transient people are physically hard on property.

Attending to the yard is not common in poverty. It takes money and skills. When the children were planting the flowers on that Sunday morning, I knew none of them possessed the skill to dig in the dirt, because not one of them was criticizing the other for not doing it right. Poverty is very talkative and very often critical and destructive in conversations. I see that as an attempt to elevate their status a little higher in social groups. The lack of procedural self-talk was very obvious, because the simplest steps had to be repeated and monitored. We spent a lot of time talking about cause and effect and logic of handling and placing the plants. The children were very responsive and after having heard the explanation and seen the demonstration, they were exceptionally gentle with the plants. And, I saw a shift in their interaction with their peers. They became mentors, filled with explanations and staged demonstrations. The energy moved from struggle to confidence. Their desire to fulfill the role of caregiver carried over through the summer. It was easy to understand the magnitude of community gardens in poverty. They are excellent mentoring moments, and they grow self-value right beside the vegetables. They create calm, quiet moments for sharing through nature in an otherwise very noisy environment.

There is a lot of noise in *The Hood*. I don't think poverty ever sleeps. In fact, when Roy and I first walked through the prison gates at GCI, we took the low noise level for granted until the black female guards started yelling across the compound at each other. Fascinating. What they were saying was insignificant and unrelated to the circumstance. It seemed it was more of a ploy for the spotlight. It was their voices that called our attention to the stark difference between male and female voices in poverty.

The female voice is generally very loud, dominant, controlling, and often angry. I believe this is centered in the inevitable loss of males to death or prison. This is the reverse of the middle class, where the male voice dominates and prestige within the social group is lost from acting out in public or presenting oneself in an unfashionable, flamboyant manner.

I have not yet spoken of the distinct clothing style of *The Hood*, or the poor. The impoverished authentically own their identity. Clearly they don't have the luxury of making up or putting on identity as the upper classes can. The middle class can go slumming as a temporary fashion statement or in rebellion against parents. There are few choices for the impoverished. However, just as I see inside prisons, there is always a way to find your individual statement even when everyone is issued the same uniform. There are acceptable variations. A lot of these variations are a reflection of what has morphed under the influence and guise of incarceration. Examples of this reflection are easily discernable to those of us who travel in both worlds. Let me give you some examples.

Tattoos are one of the storyboards that feel like individuality and can give the owner an illusion of power, toughness, or sometimes a false sense of security. They can be drawn with a contraband sewing needle, the carbon from cigarette ashes, or ink from a state-issued ball point pen, mixed with an available medium such as shampoo. A teardrop tattoo below the eye can be given in an alley or just after the rush of murdering a rival gang member. A tat that may be desirable on the streets, in the circle of a gang, can be a death wish inside prison.

When shoestrings were considered weapons and were taken away from prisoners, leaving them with unlaced Timberland boots to drag around, we began to see shoes without strings in solidarity and as a result of economic lack in the underprivileged neighborhoods. Then as it spread across classes, there was a revolution in shoe designs that ultimately generated a new manner of walking in the awkward, loose shoes. This was a necessary adaptation inside prisons also. It even came with a name: "swag."

When belts were considered weapons and were taken away from prisoners, leaving them with the continual problem of keeping their worn-out, stretched out, over-sized uniform pants pulled up, we began to see young males give up their belts and mirror the sagging. When furnishing elasticized, pull-on uniform pants became an economical advantage over regular uniform pants for prisoners, we began to see scrubs and pajama bottom pants as acceptable daily fashion on the outside.

When prisoners began to shave their heads because they couldn't afford to buy shampoo or to pay for haircuts, we saw the shaved head become an icon for being tough. We also saw the tattoos spread to the head.

The summer shirt that prisoners wear is what is termed a "wife beater." It is a deep-cut, white, sleeveless tee shirt. They are cool, comfortable, affordable, and they show off a man's muscle and tats. Again, because of their popularity in lower class cultures, they acquired their common label.

Prisoners are issued heavy sweatshirt hoodies as a staple garment that is critical for protection from the rain, cold, and wind.

They are usually navy, dark brown, dark green, or gray to avoid using gang colors. Hence, in a reflection of prison attire, everyone discovered how warm, cozy, and convenient a hoodie can be and they became a staple with most youth, and adults. However, because of their path to popularity, there is still the common attachment of evil-intentions when a black youth pulls up his hood outside of his home territory. This simple action can get a boy shot (i.e. Trayvon Martin 2012.) In fact, just wearing the wrong color in the wrong Hood can get a boy shot.

I was facilitating an Art of Trauma: Grief-Impairment class inside an Ohio prison about two years ago. The men were sharing their collages and talking about their real or perceived losses. A black man, about thirty-five years old, told the story of growing up so deeply embedded in the Crips gang of Los Angeles that he was never allowed to wear or own anything red. He said red was always his favorite color and he didn't understand why he couldn't use all of his Crayons. He felt strong enough about it that he had the loss of color on his list of losses, along with the loss of innocence.

An anthropologist's next question might be why the changes in prison show up in the impoverished cultures first, and then spread to upper class populations. The answer is obviously simple. Those are the families who sit inside the visiting rooms of prisons. Many of the young men who are visiting carry generational anger for the loss of dads, brothers, uncles, cousins, and even granddads. They know that prison is often considered "the right of passage" for their people and it's coming for them. There are a lot of emotions and solidarity. There's a feeling of carrying a little part of your dad with you when he's absent.

Mirroring prison fashion has a way of supplementing economic deficiency. For example, when sagging became acceptable, it allowed boys to wear many sizes of pants, rather than rotating one or two pair that fit properly, especially without having easy access to laundry accommodations. In a culture where survival is literal, dressing like a tough prisoner can present an illusionary shield. Then, when prisoners return home, they continue to dress in familiar, comfortable, available, affordable clothing. Middle-class logic would guess that they would want to wear anything but what they had worn in prison. However, unless the prisoner was truly GQ prior to his case and has access to money or does not return to an impoverished neighborhood, it just doesn't work that way.

People who live in *The Hood* can't afford to stand out in any way that violates their community norms. It is dangerous to rebel in an impoverished community: a complex, multi-layered danger. The phenomenon is more subconscious than the will of choice. The fight or flight mode is always plugged in and is inevitable. Freezing is not an option in *The Hood*. Staying within familiar territory is key. Survival is based on one's information, hyper-vigilance, and being ready to fight – willing to kill if necessary.

On the other hand, there is no imminent danger attached to middle-class identity choices. They are just viewed as fads or stages of development and are usually individualized with the intention of standing out in a crowd, so to speak, or in an attempt to blend in with a lower-class subculture.

Declarations of independence in behavior or identity are contra to the hidden rules of the lower classes. Impoverished people share an amazing ethic of helping each other. I saw it in my work with the homeless and with this work. I believe that is because they need each other in order to survive. They need other people in their group because survival means food, shelter, clothes, and safety; and, social groups mean resources and protection. That is why they can't afford to be competitive within their group.

In fact, I learned while facilitating a puppet program for the children of the incarcerated that it is not acceptable to give awards to individuals. The recognition must go to the team, or group. There is camaraderie, a hidden rule. It is acceptable to recognize each one as part of the group, but not to single just a few out and present them with awards. This act could put a child in danger. This is opposite to middle-class expectations.

The silent roar in poverty is survival. Real survival. The struggle to struggle. The never-ending race to stay ahead of the proverbial tiger and the ever-present trigger. When we examine where the accent on survival is placed in the middle class, it would be material-based, such as keeping the corporate job in order to keep the house and possessions. And, the accent on survival among the upper class is placed on growing the generational wealth. There are no ever-present thoughts of imminent physical danger in any class above the impoverished. These conditions and thoughts have to be taken into consideration when writing programs and theories regarding the rise out of poverty. The struggles have to be acknowledged just to get buy-in from this population. It is critical in order to fill classrooms and retain student participation.

I think it is important to touch on a major double standard within America. I have witnessed many conversations regarding this standard. The white people, or upper classes, are quick to wage war against people of other countries in order to gain territory, to defend human or civil rights, or to gain political power. But, they have a problem when impoverished American people who are struggling to survive and keep their children alive take action and wage wars over turf, democratic values, honor, or position in their world. I know highly-decorated military soldiers who have fought in hand-to-hand combat and received great accolades for killing the enemy in war. They returned to their marginalized neighborhood with hopes of mentoring the youth, but they now are serving life sentences in prison for shooting someone who was an immediate threat to them or their family. Where's the mercy? Note that the veteran prisoners groups are one of the largest inmate organizations inside the prisons.

Steve Harvey, best-selling author and television personality, wrote that a man's role is to possess, provide and protect his female and family. In poverty, a man's value is based on his ability as a lover and a fighter. If he can work hard and provide financial substance, it is an extra. Most of the men struggle to find a job with their felony records and have to depend on their female to have a job or entitlements. The shortage of legal, fulltime jobs for felons fuels the illegal drug industry. The belief drugs provide an escape from a miserable, hopeless life is even more fuel.

It appears to me most of the physical fights between men in this population are rooted in what is perceived as disrespect. I know of many men who have been shanked for something as simple as cutting in chow line. The charge is almost always "He disrespected me." It's really about one's right to exist and have self-respect and public esteem. Words and events that don't even make the radar of the middle class build up like grains of sand on beaches and then, in one quick moment, the switch flips and all hell breaks loose. The straw breaks the camel's back. The percolated explosion isn't personal, it is inevitable. It is a manifestation of repressed issues and incidents. It is the result of a man allowing himself to indulge in things that he does or doesn't want to do and then justifying his actions as necessary for survival. I hear stories over and over about how the little boy wanted to be one thing, but the only choices and models he saw were poverty and crime. The prisoners who spend their prison time improving their social and educational assets always have goals for high achievement and service to others when they return to community. But, the many challenges of reentry and employment for felons are often bigger than the goals, and the individuals fall back to what is familiar, if even for the proverbial one time. It is difficult to believe in happy endings under those circumstances.

Drugs, alcohol, gambling, smoking are all chronic cycles of addiction to numb the emotions and feelings that crowd a man's mind in this fight to survive in a world where one's contributions and needs are not valued because of color or perceived personal failures. They are also hooks that can lock one into believing it's all tied into survival. Humans can get caught up in cycles of attachment that look like safety, but are actually just masks to cover up the denial of parts of oneself. Based on the environment where one grew up, humans, as intelligent, adaptive creatures, learn what they have to do to survive. This becomes their primary set of values. Their model. We must have an idea of their model if we are to affect cyclic change.

Chapter Three
FROM ART TO ANALYSIS INSIDE PRISONS

Ohio House Bills 113 and 131 (2007) had just been passed, and ODRC and state dignitaries held formal community forums at all of the prisons for the purpose of extending an invitation to the community churches and non-profit organizations to bring programs into the prisons. The public volunteers were to help prepare the prisoners for reentry back into community. The prisons were, and still are, operating dangerously above capacity and corrections had turned their attention to resolving the issue of recidivism in order to address the budget reductions that were sweeping the state and nation. The speakers cited the fact that 51% of the prisoners were serving time for non-violent crimes, and 95% of the prisoners would reenter their community, whether their community was ready or not. They told us that they recognized that the ODRC is not the easiest group of people to work with, but that they needed us to keep trying; because they needed help from community organizations.

So, my procedural entrance into the Ohio prisons came as the gates were opened to community. This happened dramatically before the staff had been psychologically habituated to the presence of outsiders inside a formerly closed institution, where two thousand plus prisoners lived without direct contact with anyone other than family or staff. This was a huge paradigm shift and it felt like a loaded cannon. Everyone seemed to be hyper-focused on everyone else.

Stepping into the subcultures of prison is like going to the back side of the mirror. Everything flips, including many academic theories. All the rules and expectations are foreign to the people entering prison life. The hidden rules, founded in paranoia and control, are difficult to translate. They are more reaction-based, and are heavily weighted with historical context. Logic defies definition under the auspex of corrections. And time - time crawls as if it runs backward. If I've learned any one absolute thing over these seven years, it's this: all things remain plausible and possible inside prison walls. And, I might add, you just never know whom you'll run into while you're there.

In life, I am an extremist and a warrior, but in this arena, I was very much a novice setting sail in uncharted waters. I was fortunate to have three liberal, legendary wardens to mold and guide me: Khelleh Konteh, Dennis Baker, and Richard Hall. Their words were direct, insightful, and supportive. As I look back on those first three years, I now realize that they had placed a virtual cloak around me and charged me with bringing change to their prisons. They called me a "breath of fresh air" and would continually challenge me to create programs of merit. They handpicked twenty prisoners to be my core group within each select prison and we did the work together as a team. It was as if the prisons were a lab and we were united in constructing the experiments that we felt would be most beneficial for that population. We piloted program after program. We continued to tweak, add and subtract until the team felt the program was working for the betterment of the population, based on signup and retention numbers and decrease of behavior tickets for the students.

Successful programs are built to counter the environmental and cultural damages, and to develop or awaken self-value. Therefore, having a reasonably keen sense of what that looks like is critical for writing program curriculum. They have to be culturally sensitive if they are to remain effective over time. A writer, and teacher, must be aware of the cultural damage the prisoner presents at the time of his entrance into prison, and, additionally, what common damage the prison environment itself can cause for the prisoner.

The prison environment is incomprehensible. Even after almost a decade of going through the gates, the sally port still feels like a shape-shifting portal to prepare for the other side of the wall – residents and staff and time. Not so obvious to outsiders, there is more stress between staff persons than between staff and prisoners. As a survival-among-peers measure in an ever-revolving setting, the players silently assess and sort one another as "lovers, haters, or pretenders." "Lovers" are the humanitarians who see inmates as people. "Haters" are the individuals who see inmates as unsalvageable degenerates who should be caged and castigated. "Pretenders" are individuals who pretend to be "lovers," but are really "haters." The "pretenders" are not so easily identified as they often befriend the "lovers" in order to be taken into confidence. They stock information to use later for personal gain and control; playing both sides of the game. This was first explained to me in detail by a seasoned staff member who had invited me to spend the day shadowing her inside a prison. As we moved through the day, she identified and labeled staff. She was adamant about not trusting anyone. I carry her words with me. I watch the stress, the flow of tattle-tale stories, the eyes watching eyes, the emotions and fear that loom just below the surface, burning away at the souls.

Adrenaline runs through prisons like water in mighty rivers. People, prisoner or not, who spend much time within the walls will more than likely get caught up in the gamble and the rush of it. It's turned on when people get caught, almost get caught, or are worried about getting caught. It's turned on by sneaking, by breaking rules, or by watching others break the rules, especially recurrently as individuals or in group. Everyone has some blackmail-worthy data on everyone else: obscure control.

It's primarily turned on by unethical or inhumane acts towards other people. By exhibitionism or voyeurism. Showmanship. The buttons are not always sexual, but frequently are. It's a cat and mouse game that always gets out of hand and always causes damage, mostly psychological. Mostly permanent. So troubling and emotionally mutilating that many clear-sighted leaders seek the blueprint that would guide humanity out of this malignant maze. The psychological and emotional fallout of the intense games spills over into all facets of the players' lives. Amusement and dares at work morph into lifestyle, and the delineation between work and personal life quickly fades and character veils are ripped apart.

After work, when the uniform comes off, the guilt and psychological damages resulting from hostile behavior towards volunteers, peers, and those in one's charge will always take its full toll. Hostility is like a wildfire, burning out of control, all consuming. Hostility creates escalading stress for both the antagonist and the target. It shows up in addictions to alcohol, drugs, sex, gambling, and domestic violence. It destroys intimate relationships and divides families as surely as Moses divided the Red Sea. Few marriages or families can withstand the predictable, widespread repercussions of a member working inside a prison. And after the family is gone, who can the person relate to outside incarceration? It's like a mighty quicksand.

Adrenaline is also turned on by humane acts of compassion, affection, or friendship, all of which are frowned upon by the commanding system and considered evidence of forming a prohibited relationship with an inmate. In the literal translation of prison policy, inmates are to be given nothing, are not to be touched, and are to know nothing personal about staff or civilians. Such action can be interpreted as a rule infraction and the performer can be permanently walked off the property and subjected, along with any inmates perceived as participants, to a lengthy investigation. In fact, staff or civilians can get away with punitive, demeaning actions toward inmates much more readily than acts of consideration or kindness. Being mean is expected. Being kind is considered a red flag.

To be clear, some actions and interactions can appear to be affectionate in nature, when a closer, broader examination would identify them as manipulative and taunting. In a world where humans are deprived of touch and intimate relationships, a female guard who walks through the male showers, making affectionate comments or touches as she glides through, can spoil a man's sexual health.

This scenario of females in male prisons and males in female prisons can be every bit as deep and perverted as a mind can wonder, and I will leave it there. However, I must include the recurring phenomenon of female prisoners having babies when they weren't pregnant at the time they entered prison. There's a nursery inside the prison that houses the babies for eighteen months, and then they are separated from their mothers. Now who's the victim?

It is important to note the severity of the permanent mental and sexual damage that is created by such an environment, even vicariously. Many forms of nooky are readily

available inside prisons. I think we cannot
be so haughty as to think that we can force
abstinence upon people just because they
are in prison. People are creative. Can you
honestly see yourself remaining totally
isolated and deprived of intimacy and
validation for years – honestly? Consider this
at the same time you consider that any form
or sembalance of masturbation is prohibited
inside prisons and is punished as a serious
infraction. However, I am told that there is
a double standard in place at the female
prisons because the guards are more
commonly male.

It is easy to turn from these things and
declare that the actions and situations that
I have observed are not real, or certainly do
not apply to the majority. To that, I submit
the well-known 1971 Stanford Prison
Experiment which was designed to examine
the effects that uniforms, group think, and
authority have on individuals placed in a
simulated prison. The two-week experiment
escaladed severely and was cancelled after
six days. Simplified, the study concluded
people will embrace the personification of
the uniform they wear; however, it is
tempered or magnified by the individual's
sense of moral identity. In other words, the
degree to which a person understands how
their actions affect others, or the whole, will
determine their ethical behavior, and
whether they choose to go with what's

morally right or their innate aggressiveness. I would submit humans have a strong tendency to project or inflict punishment to the degree they secretly feel they themselves deserve: harbored guilt, perhaps. I identify this as a complication of the shadow effect.

So, when you combine the rush of adrenaline with uniformed staff and put them into a position of power over a marginalized, forgotten, imprisoned population, you can bank on unhealthy results for all involved. Especially since the imprisoned are also wearing uniforms and are struggling to remember their own identity - and to resist their street urge to defend themselves. Often what prevents their outburst is the fact that they have no one to tell or to defend them. They feel hopeless, and the prison medical plan is not weighted in their favor.

The Stanford Experiment identified three types of guards: tough but fair and rule abiding; good guys who granted favors and did not punish; and hostile guards who had no limit on their creative forms of prisoner humiliation and punishment. I would argue the authentic good guy guard would quickly become oppressed by vicarious trauma from the effect of what he witnessed and would cycle out of the job pretty quickly.

Currently, the entry position of correction

guard requires a sixth-grade education equivalency. I find that to be disturbing criteria since they are the frontline authority who establish the model and the atmosphere of the prisons. Because of their history of lower education – probably generational - they tend to see no value in prison programming and are inclined to sabotage such efforts and any outside facilitators. There are anomalies, but as a matter of course, it amuses them to destroy what perplexes them most: positive programming to help prepare prisoners for successful reentry back into community. This atmosphere does put a noticeable strain on facilitators who are not state staff, and I find it takes a lot of stamina, fortitude, and persistence to continue to teach inside. This is further curious when one considers that ODRC will pay for employees' education.

This struggle to deliver positive programming to prisoners relates to a statement a former director of the ODRC shared with me during one of our many visits. He said a third of the prisoners "got" the lesson as soon as they heard the first steel prison gate slam behind them. They could have been returned to community right then and would have never committed another crime.

He said one-third of the prisoners are so damaged they will have to be locked up for the rest of their lives, and there's nothing we can do to alter the damage enough to make them fit to reenter community. But he continued to explain, society needs to be accountable for the damage that culminated, in part, in who these people became and their treatment in prison should be humane. They are still people; even prisoners on death row are still people.

It's the last third we have to focus on, he continued. Their outcome is based on their prison experience, which is why positive programs are so critical inside prisons. He also said he felt twenty percent of the fifty thousand prisoners who are incarcerated in Ohio are innocent. This comes from a man whose job required him to set aside his personal beliefs and facilitate and witness executions.

At the end of his term, the budget cuts had dictated changes in prison program policies. Only prisoners who were five years or less to the gate (release) are now allowed to participate in educational programs, including earning a GED. That meant many prisoners who would spend their days in a classroom were not eligible to do so. More unhealthy idleness. Educational staff was cut back. Approximately ten percent of Ohio prisoners are actually in programs now. Ten percent! The anatomy of prisons is highly complicated and indecipherable. It is ever-morphing and the more it shows its under-belly, the more it requires in return. It is a fertile ground to grow pre-existing or dormant personality traits.

If one has any sadistic, deviant tendencies, it will magnify them and encourage seeking out and feeding on the deviations of the captive population. This applies to anyone inside the walls. It can transform an ordinary individual into a willing perpetrator or victim of evil. If one has a good and strong sense of divine self-value and the oneness of humanity, then they are less likely to succumb to the corruption of power and authority. Their actions and reactions will more often be structured as guidance, leadership, and teaching opportunities as opposed to dehumanization of prisoners. They will tend to promote human values rather than destroy them. My observation is that healthy moral identity is usually a reflection of an individual's pursuit of higher education and spirituality. It just makes sense to me that the state would readily allocate educational funds for both employees and prisoners. In the bigger picture, I strongly believe it would pay for itself on many levels.

Speaking of cutting costs and being good stewards of state funds, a big question I've always had is why prisoners who are given a death sentence are put into solitary confinement for decades. This is very expensive and both the prisoners and the staff are living in excessive stress due to the inhumane operations of the elaborate and expensive environment created to prevent human contact. Is there a fear the prisoner might be killed if left in general population? Death sentences are usually handed out in murder cases; most murderers are given life sentences and they are walking around in the general population of the prison. Not to mention, I believe the statistic is three out of ten executed prisoners are posthumously found to be innocent.

The expense incurred to isolate prisoners is often passed on to their committing county. Honestly, isolation seems to be very extravagant and unnecessary on many levels, especially considering that the exorbitant monies required to unnecessarily segregate human beings inside prisons could be used to battle one of the largest and most serious grassroots problems driving incarceration: ineffective educational systems. Illiteracy runs rampant among prisoners, who are predominantly haptic learners. It runs rampant in our juveniles and our adults.

In an illiterate subculture, the arts typically flourish as a means of self-expression. So I was a good fit with a bachelor's degree in fine arts, a minor in psychology, and three years of helping to facilitate art programs with an overflowing homeless population in

New Mexico. Thus, I began my work inside the prison walls as a therapeutic art teacher. My first workshops were on color theory, print making, and handmade books. And, following the publication of my third book, The Retablo Affect, I was asked to facilitate a workshop where the men would be guided on "getting through the garbage to the God inside themselves," followed by an iconic self-portrait.

The Retablo Affect was written as a result of my learning the seventeenth-century folk art of painting Catholic saints in a very primitive style called Retablo. The beloved art form was created by the Spanish pilgrims who were left to settle the New Mexico area and to convert the Native American Indians over to Catholicism. The Spaniards were left without master artists to paint their beloved saints and out of desperation they gathered – from the surrounding land – gypsum, rabbit skin glue, poplar wood planks, pinion tree sap, plant, bug, and mineral pigments. And, with the guidance of the local Native American Indian rug weavers who knew how to stabilize natural pigments as light-fast dye, they created the beloved folk art. They discovered that if they could paint a simple human figure and capture the icons and symbolisms that represent each individual saint, then they would have their spiritual artifacts to hang on their walls and place on their alters. Being without them would be sacrilegious.

As a metaphysician who had just begun
to explore artifacts of Catholicism, I began
reading many books, looking at the history
and stories of the many Catholic saints and
wondering how many were real and how
many were created to control the masses.
There would have naturally been
embellishments added to any story over
the centuries, a distinct pattern of attaching
significant symbols and icons to figures to
represent that saint's story. As I studied, my
mind began to wonder about everyone's life
symbols and icons that have significant
representation of the purpose that runs
through their life. The core of their being.
The pattern that everyone but the subject
person seems to see.

If we accept the premise that God made all
human beings, then every human life would
logically be given purpose and would
inherently identify and attach to certain
symbols and patterns that would represent or
resonate with that purpose. Scriptures do tell
us that God - by many names - is
omnipresent, omniscient, and omnipotent.
As I understand it, that means that everything
that is, is made out of and by God. Because
we are eternal spirit beings having corporeal
experiences on this plane, our lives also
inherently attach to a lot of human-
generated garbage that conceals the

presence of God. The very nature of this paradigm clouds and distorts the divine worth and value of the individual eternal essence or soul, which cannot be tarnished or destroyed. I call this "divine self-value." So, if we can get through the garbage to the God presence in ourselves, then we can more readily see God in others, and in our environment. That makes sense to me and it is the core premise of The Retablo Affect.

The prisoners themselves asked me to bring The Retablo Affect workshop into the prisons and to guide them through exercises that would awaken or renew their self-value and restore hope to their lives. Without hope, the prisoners will really struggle to succeed at reentering family or community upon release, and they'll likely recidivate. The workshops were well-received and found to be effective.

During this same period, I was attending graduate classes at Kent State University. I wrote a Sociology of Religion paper that earned me an A+ and motivated me to ask the warden to let me work with a group of twelve sage prisoners to review and test my theories and assumptions. The title of the paper was *An Analysis of Religion inside Male Prisons as a Predictor of Recidivism*. I prepared a 28-page questionnaire and allotted two Friday sessions of four hours to prove my paper. It read beautifully and was filled with intertwining social and psychological theories. I thought it was brilliant.

I am here to tell you, that nothing went as planned. As soon as the men figured out that our space was safe for "truth-telling," they had a lot to say about the theories and assumptions I had written. They had questions! Most of the patterns I was so sure I would find were not there. Most of the theories I cited were flipped upside down or dissolved. All I had embraced as exceptional on my part held no merit by the end of our four-month discussion every Friday. There weren't even enough surviving chards to support a rewrite. I finally threw my arms up and declared we had beaten it up enough and I guessed we were done, finished. I'd see them all in the next art workshop.

With that, one of the younger men spoke up and suggested I wasn't going anywhere; I was going to teach them. The other eleven echoed his sentiments. They said we had met in that room at 8 o'clock on Friday mornings for so long the prison had begun to refer to the space as Ms. Briney's room. I raised an eyebrow and asked "What am I going to teach you?" I was told to come back the next Friday and we would figure it out; that they had come to know me and how I thought well enough to know I could teach them many things. Well, okay then.

We met and brainstormed our strategy over the next two Fridays. At the end of the second week, we had a chalkboard literally filled with words and topics that were being considered for classes. As the team was leaving, I said we had to decide. I had to plan. Which word was it going to be? What was I going to teach? The same young man who had originally spoken up about my teaching walked up, took the chalk out of my hand, circled two separate words - sociology and metaphyics - and handed the chalk back to me as he walked towards the exit door to head to his bunk for count-time.

I asked "Which one?" and his reply was "Both. Think about it. See you Friday." I stood there thinking how bizarre the idea was. How could I put those two topics together? It turned out to be a cutting-edge idea.

The next Friday, we talked about their vision. I needed to hear what they wanted most to pull out of my brain. What did they see in me that gave them hope and direction? We formed a big circle with our school desks, and we talked and discussed for four more weeks, three hours every Friday. The end product was a mission statement and a twenty-week curriculum that combined social theories, ontological questions, and applied metaphysics. We entitled the course The Empowerment of Socio-Metaphysics. We also decided that I would reach out to guest speakers to address the weekly classes, in hopes that some of them would be brave enough to come into the prison. We never, in our wildest dream, expected that everyone I invited to speak would welcome the opportunity and would continue to come into multiple prisons with me.

Socio-Met became my signature course and Warden Hall said that we had managed to change the conversation on the compound. I placed my personal metaphysics library of over 200 books on loan to the prison. I told the chair of the Kent Sociology department about our courses and, in support of our endeavors, he gathered and donated over three hundred books from his department professors. The socio-metaphysics library has now grown to just under a thousand books.

Metaphysics, simply stated, is the utilization of science, theology, sociology, psychology, history, anthropology, spirituality, quantum physics, and alternative modalities to explore the ontological questions of life, purpose, and death. The actual impact of the course is that students learn deductive reasoning. They are encouraged to question everything. They examine their own core and *a priori* beliefs. They learn to examine their purpose and roles in eternal time sequences: that where they are has positive value and opportunity for them.

When I first started writing and facilitating prison programs, I was told by ODRC that self-esteem and self-value-based-programs had no merit in reducing recidivism. The programs had to be cognitive behavior, daily literacy, reentry readiness, or vocational in order to be effective. Since then, words like holistic, self-value, and healing are often used in the context of reentry reintegration, programming, and grant language. I will always argue you can give a man three million dollars, exonerate him of crimes and release him from prison. But, if he doesn't comprehend his universal self-value, he will self-sabotage and likely lose it all, maybe even cycle back into crime and even prison. Man must grasp the concept of his purpose and his impact on the greater good of humanity in order to embrace his own greater good. There is a big difference between success and fulfillment.

Having learned of our success with socio-metaphysics classes in 2008, the ODRC director had asked me to create a course to address the grief and loss that shadows all prisoners. It took me two years to get the courage to open that can of worms, so to speak. I feared I would bring up unresolved emotions that would drive violence or suicide and I'd not be on property to work with my students. However, after a long conversation with a sage who had served over thirty years, his words encouraged me to move forward.

He said "Ms. Briney, you don't have to worry about opening a can of worms. The emotions, visions, details, smell, sounds, remorse of our case and our lives never left. Every time we close our eyes, it's all right there. It never changes or leaves. You could only help us."

When this program was first launched, we called it The Art of Grief-Impairment. It was such a new frontier with so many unknown factors that we literally created it as we went. The best medium for the course was altered books. We took old hardback books and altered them by cutting six pages out, leaving six, cutting six, leaving six. Participants could then sew, brad, or glue the six remaining pages into one signature page. That provided them a bound series of canvases onto which they could build healing collages. It also gave them a tangible history that they could hold and examine.

Each week, something would show up in the men's discussions that would give me clarity for the next assignment. The guys would create an assigned collage and the next week I would present them with an exercise corresponding to the collage. By the time we were halfway through the second twenty week class, there were distinct patterns that were showing up around the losses that the prisoners had experienced and how they were affected by them.

They would say things like "I was young.
Mom and Dad got a divorce. Dad left. We
moved in with Grandma. Grandma died,
and I wasn't prepared to handle that. So, I
started acting out. And here I am." During
a quiet moment in class, as everyone was
working on their books one day, a man just
blurted out "My Daddy shot and killed
himself when I was five. I should have gotten
the gun out of the car." Another was "My big
brother got shot. If I had been there, I could
have helped him." A common one, "My
stepdad would come home drunk, duct
tape me to the basement pole, and burn
me with his cigarettes, or beat me." "I was
raped" seems to be as common among
male children as female children.

There were many parallels and coincidences.
We became aware there were traumas that
happened early in the childhood of these
men. Sometimes there was so much abuse
that they had become desensitized. As a
child, they usually had no one to go to, one
who had the coping skills to guide them.
Nothing to do but act out their feelings. We
became aware that in this classroom space
where, together, we had created a feeling
of safety, men were willing to return to their
childhood and reexamine what had
happened to them. They have to go back
to the trauma, the place where they are

stuck in life. Like in the movie <u>Goodwill Hunting</u>, this class is all about understanding and knowing "It's not your fault." It's about healing the childhood trauma. It's about sharing experiences with other people and finding self-value when they receive it and heal with you.

Until a friend started telling me about Judge Michael Howard's writings on trauma-informed care, I thought we had made a new discovery. I was excited to know there were professionals who were ahead of me and I could study their work. I knew we had to reframe the childhood trauma by looking at it through the lens of the man today if we were to ever alter or stop the emotional acting out. We have to help them to get unstuck.

These unresolved traumas often result in arrested development, both socially and psychologically – fostering addictions. One student reflected on the hopelessness of being stuck: "The negative realm is our realm and we prepare ourselves for it." So, we began to examine what can make the difference in whether a person thinks positively or negatively. Certainly blame and accountability can impact that.

Trauma-informed care - which asks "what happened to you?" instead of "what did you do?" - is a societal shift in blame that can restore self-value and open a person to emotional growth and positive forward thinking. So, trauma-informed care became the methodology of the course. We renamed it The Art of Trauma: Grief-Impairment. Students use magazine images to collage their list of perceived, tangible or intangible losses inside their altered books. They are also guided to collage childhood dreams and longings so they can remember their innocence. The closing collage is about their future dreams. They embellish pages with stickers, glitter, paint, sketches, handmade papers, and family photos. The books become animated treasure troves that bear witness to the student's life history. Students are allowed to keep them at their bunk, or to carry them into a visit where they can share them with, even gift them to, family members.

Whenever I meet with wardens for the first time, I asked them to describe the program they carry around in their head. If they could just wave a magic wand and bring it to fruition at their prison, what program do they feel would really help their prison population? That was how our Mentoring through Erudition (MTE) program was birthed. Warden Bennie Kelly wanted a certificated program where the prisoners could mentor each other through education. He wanted a program that would assess the skills, talents, and education of prisoners and have the infrastructure for them to teach one another in classroom settings and include a formal graduation ceremony.

The MTE program was in conflict with ODRC policy which states that one prisoner is not to have power over another prisoner. However, a warden has the power to bend policy at his compound. So we began the lengthy process of creating a mini-college out of thin air. There were twenty prison leaders in our core group. We used Youngstown State University, Kent State University, and ODRC rules, regulations, and school documents to create all of the forms and syllabuses. The men evaluated every limitation and expectation and then tweaked them to what they felt was more reasonable and inspirational for the students.

Then we set about discovering who we could call upon to teach. At first, I thought we would canvas the compound population to find the teachers. Then I realized the teachers were in the room with me. When I had that epiphany, I went around the room asking "If you had to teach a class today, what would it be?" and they all gave me a quick answer.

We originally called the program <u>Mentoring through Education</u>, but the prison principal - who laughed at the concept and said there wasn't a prisoner out there who had more than a sixth-grade education - started making waves about the program being under her control. That would have been most unhealthy, so we quickly changed the E to Erudition; which means knowledge acquired through study or research. And, as it all turns out, erudition was a much better fit. Some of the prisoners had formal education, even doctorates, but mostly they teach topics they are passionate about and have self-taught over the years. These college-level classes are interesting and challenging.

The greatest impact of MTE is it replaces idleness with positive programming and mentoring opportunities that do not have out-time restrictions on them. Because the classes are co-facilitated by two prisoners who cannot be "played," only the serious students enroll in the classes. MTE is a perfect venue for "each one teach one." After almost four years, it is easy to see self-value is felt by the core group, the instructors, the assistant instructors, and the administrative aides who work together as a tight team to make this program run year round. We average twenty classes of fifteen men (small classrooms) per twenty-week semester.

A very important latent benefit of MTE is it provides the men with a new dialog to discuss with their friends and families on the phone, in letters, and in the visiting room.

New knowledge brings self-value, especially when it is a gift to your family or someone you are mentoring. These new discussions breathe life into people. The men are able to bring new knowledge to the conversations about finances, music, health, science, poetry, philosophy, sustainable agriculture, grief processing, publishing, and many more subjects.

Because I have published a two-volume anthology of prisoner writings - The Prison Coffee Table Book Project - I receive a lot of requests from national prisoners who are seeking publication of their manuscripts. After many false starts to resolve this quandary, I was given a space within a prison to set up the Prison Publication Center (PPC) where prisoners would help with the selection of manuscripts, edit and type them, illustrate them, and prepare them to be published and sold through Amazon. com. This allowed us to provide a wonderful, free service to talented writers, which encouraged them to continue to write from their prison cells.

The PPC created a space where prisoners could learn computer, editing, and illustration skills, as well as work as a team in support of fellow writers. This space, with three computers, also serves for convenient and expanded support of curriculum documents and class attendance tallies for the other RBN classes at that prison. The PPC was one of the first settings where prisoners were allowed to work on computers. This was a monumental event which set a precedent for the warden to create a space in the library where prisoners could work on legal documents. It was a sure sign that policies were progressively changing.

After about four years of creating individual certificated programs, we designed the RBN Excellence Program. It allows students to matriculate through seven courses over an eighteen-month period: Introduction to Prison Programming; Self-Development for Successful Reentry, based on Dr. Phil Amerine's work; Financial Peace University based on Dave Ramsey's work; Empowerment of Socio-Metaphysics; Advanced Applied Socio-Metaphysics; Art of Trauma: Grief Impairment; and, Understanding Poverty, based on Dr. Ruby Payne's work.

Dr. Ruby Payne's work on poverty is some of the most outstanding and valuable work I have found. Throughout this essay I have mentioned "hidden rules," which are a direct reference to her writings. Her analyses and theories are so powerful and enlightening that we teach directly from her book A Framework for Understanding Poverty (2005). It answers the question "What difference does it make how I talk?" Students become aware of the different language registries and hidden rules of the classes and we discuss how they can improve their living, education, and working status just by improving their language awareness and skills.

Payne breaks down the five language registries and explains why impoverished people struggle in school, business, banking, parent-teacher conferences, courtrooms, reentry requirements, etc. All of those institutions are founded on middle-class formal language registry that has a consecutive discourse, while poverty speaks in a much more casual, meandering, entertaining registry. Thus, there's a profound communication breakdown between the cultures and, hence, poverty loses. Even poverty that wins the lottery will often not maintain wealth beyond a minute because the language barriers and hidden rules of the middle class and wealthy will defeat them and dissolve the fortune.

There are many prisoners who spend their prison time retooling themselves by reading and studying. Hence, their language is upgraded to middle class registry. This often generates ridicule from family and friends. They accuse them of trying to talk and be like the white people. We caution students not to get caught up in this criticism. Family and friends are just saying those things because they don't know how to deal with the individual's education. They aren't sure how it effects their relationship – Does it make them look stupid?

I have already spoken of the rampant illiteracy in the prison population. Many have a very limited vocabulary, especially in the 18-to-25 year-old group. There are many theories on why it is more specific to this group, but that would be another chapter. The fact is these young men do not have enough vocabulary to say what they are feeling, wanting, or thinking. In addition, they are used to using body language and hand signs to help express where their words leave them at a loss. Their language registry is very casual, mixed with what Payne terms intimate registry. We have added a sixth registry to depict the prison registry. We call it nadir, the lowest point of language.

The 18-25 year-old group is highly emotional and have often not had stable mentors or seen positive modeling. They are volatile. This does not mean the individuals are stupid. It means they can't express themselves effectively or sufficiently. This will always lead to frustration and acting out – usually violently. Hence, having a successfully sponsored and run Toastmasters or Gavel Club inside every prison becomes more and more important. The question is: How do we inspire these young people to join such a club? How do we get buy-in? Without buy-in, the acting out accelerates wherever the individuals live. Without buy-in, recidivism accelerates. And, we are reminded again just how difficult this work of changing the severe generational cycles of crime and incarceration are.

Chapter Four
THE MOMENTS AND CONCLUSIONS

Over the course of my years of teaching and walking with prisoners, I have indeed had some experiences that are etched in my very being. I found them to be far more profound than I could have ever anticipated. I hope I am able to capture the spiritual and emotional depth of each event I have chosen to share in this chapter.

Couch Moment

During the four days at Grafton, I met a young black man who stood out among the crowd. He was serving a life sentence and he seemed to be so out of place. I was so perplexed by his presence in prison that I inquired of one of the elder prisoners, whom I had become more acquainted with, why this young man was in prison. His story was the first of hundreds of personal stories that have burned themselves onto my middle-class heart and memory. Stories I couldn't have even fathomed prior to walking with this population of people. It went something like this.

His mother was a heroin addict. She provided sex in exchange for drugs. In an attempt to keep a close eye on her baby boy while performing fellatio on her drug supplier, she would set the baby on the couch beside them. As soon as the boy was old enough to rescue his mom, he did. It was his ultimate primal goal as her oldest child, as a male. This meant he connected with a gang early on. The game was drugs, turf, sex, family, money and --- guns. He was in a gang shoot-out and is now in prison for life. I saw him in the visiting room six months later with a young mother and two children. He was so gentle and loving to them.

It is easy to understand this young man's path through life. It was logical modeling from where he grew and walked. It was what he saw: there is trauma behind every crime. Hurt people, hurt people. I struggled so much with this. Society constructs the self, and the self suffers the punishment and isolation. At what point did this baby have a chance? What do we do to stop this cycle?

Visiting Room Moment

I was sitting in a prison visiting room with a friend, just catching up on things, when in walked a tall, thin, aged woman wearing a full-length mink coat. She was accompanied by two men in expensive dark suits. She bore a likeness to several Hollywood icons, but most especially Kathryn Hepburn in her seventies. Everyone became silent and looked up at this highly unlikely trio. Just then the guards brought in a prisoner who couldn't have been more than eighteen. He was very thin, vulnerable, and his skin was pale against the orange jump suit he was wearing. He was shackled and chained around his wrists, ankles, and waist, as if his hundred and ten pound body might possibly escape the grip of his handlers. He was disoriented and he was sobbing like a lost baby. The guards were going to put him behind glass for his visit, but the emotions were so intense, and this woman was not the normal visitor, that the female guard motioned for them to sit him at a regular table. By this time, the woman had walked up to him and placed her hands on the sides of his face, and she was weeping as I'd never seen before, or since. She motioned to unshackle his arms, and they did. He curled up around her in an all-encompassing hug and as a child he begged her to help him. He was like a five year old who had been sacrificed to the darkest world and had only a few minutes of light left. It was such a revelation of prison that the guards didn't even know how to emotionally deal with it.

The woman looked up to the heavens and prayed for strength, as her whole body and soul bore the weight of this horrific sorrow. Tears continued to flood her face. She, once again, had to be the strong, steadfast matriarch and she knew she was powerless to change this game board. She knew she would have to leave him behind, and, perhaps, this was the last time she would see him – due to age and distance. The suited men stood there, all knowing.

The visit was short because the intensity was more than hearts can bear, and the guards literally pried the young man off of her. He wailed and begged as they practically carried him out of the visiting room: "Please take me home. Why can't I go home?" She had turned to walk away when she took the arm of one of the men to lean on, and she didn't allow herself to look back.
Needless to say, there was not a dry eye in the visiting room that day. That day when prison reached outside of poverty for its prey. A hundred or so of us, both prisoners and visitors, were witnesses. None of the prisoners seemed to know who he was or of his situation. But we all knew the cloak of sorrow and reality of incarceration were too real for any soul to remain austere. Just recalling this

long enough to write about it has me reliving too much of the experience.

Heinous Moment

It was a typical Monday morning, as I headed toward the mental health building where our MTE classes were held each week. As I approached the door, one of the core team sages opened the door and asked me to immediately meet with him and three other sages before we geared up for classes. I said sure, and we went straight to finding a room where we could talk privately.

I was braced to handle difficult logistics or to hear requests to aid someone who had gone to the hole without due process, but I couldn't have even imagined the conversation that ensued.

They began, with great and troubled emotional restraint, to tell me about an eighteen-year-old prisoner who had just recently arrived at the prison, and was assigned to their cell block. The young man had bludgeoned his mother to death with a bat. He was on drugs and she told him to turn off the video games and clean his room. He went crazy and was sentenced to life in prison.

He had come to them for consolation. They said he carries a Bible around with him all the

time and never misses a church meeting.
He told them he reads his Bible all the time,
and prays, but he cannot find a place in his
head to live with his crime. He said he was
exhausted from trying and he felt suicide
would be the only way to quiet the voices
and the visions that never go away.

As they each one took turns adding
fragments to the story, they lost their battle to
hold back tears in front of me. Their emotions
were so deep and they were so desperate
to find whatever it was they had come to me
for.

I asked what it was they wanted from me.

They began to explain they are aware when
certain prisoners are transferring into the
prison. If they have that information, then
they can be prepared to help them. To
council with them. To mentor them. They
continued to tell me they weren't successfully
finding the answer to this young man's
torment. I couldn't decipher why they were
asking me; they have far more wisdom and
experience with these things than I'll ever
have. What could I possibly bring?

They continued to try to lead me deeper into
the realities of their lives together, how to
survive one's own hell. It was hard. We kept
exchanging short chards of conversation
and questions. Then one of them said the

most profound thing to me. It had been emotionally consuming, but finally the words surfaced.

"Ms. Briney, you don't understand. You see, we all are one. You even teach us that. In here, we have to find a way to live with ourselves, to make sense out of our actions. We have to find a way to forgive ourselves. We have to find purpose in our lives. We can't just quit living. So, you see, if we are all one, then he is us, and we are him. If we can't help him find a way to live with his actions, then we can't live with ours. There is no division. We have to help him find the love, the oneness, his purpose - or we can't go on either. If he commits suicide, then we all die and we have come to you for help, because we can't bear that. Ms. Briney, we need you to come into the philosophy class as a guest speaker and just talk. We hope and believe that you will say something that will make a difference and get us all through this. Please, Ms. Briney. He won't know we talked to you."

I sat back in my chair and looked into the face of every one of them, these men who had been down twenty to thirty-five years. I got it. In the outside world, when a man kills another person, he is despised and condemned. He is isolated and even put to death. He is condemned to hell for eternity, with no bridge back. But, inside prison, there are groups of men who know about these perpetrators and they are busy preparing a place for them to continue to live. Preparing to bring them in. Preparing with honest love, not illusion of perfection. Unconditional love, understanding and acceptance. An understanding that there's an inner self who isn't that behavior. Preparing to nurture them back to the point where they can find themselves and their purpose. These men really do understand the oneness of humanity and the spiritual lessons that life brings us. They understand there are many paths and they are willing to guide and mentor the "worst of the worst" in a world that has no such consideration.

"Okay. I don't know what I'll say. Don't point him out to me. I don't want to single him out with my eyes." And I walked into the classroom and began to present metaphysical theories regarding ontological questions. I talked for a hour and a half and the twenty students were encouraged to ask questions throughout my talk. I was shooting from the hip and praying that somehow my rambling would resonate.

After class, the men have to go to their cells and be counted and go to lunch. So, I had to wait for nearly three hours to get the download from the sages. A long, solemn wait for me.

The sages reported that the young man said my talk did help him. When asked what specifically, he responded, "The part where she explained 'You are so much more than the most heinous thing you have ever done. You were created by God and you have purpose, but now you know you are accountable to yourself for what you do.'"

Cemetery Moment

From the many discussions I've been privy to, I'd say dying inside prison is the biggest fear of prisoners, young and old alike. They don't necessarily fear death; they just don't want to die inside prison and never be free. They don't want to be buried in a potter's field in a cardboard coffin, with only an ODRC number to identify the grave.

While taking a course in the sociology of death and dying, I had the opportunity to interview two prisoners who had served beyond three decades each. These men used to be the prison gravediggers and seemed relieved to be able to talk about some of the burials. During each three-hour interview, I heard many stories, so I will just pick portions that should capture the essence of their experiences.

The cemetery is between the two prisons, just outside the walls, in a lower-lying area where the water table is high and the rain accumulates. Men have been buried there for over a century and a half. The markers are broken or no longer there. God only knows if the oldest records have withstood time.

There were always two gravediggers, one guard, and just one shovel. There was no rope or strap to lower the coffin into the hole. The guard didn't want to risk the two prisoners attacking him with two shovels, tying him up and escaping.

One man would dig with the shovel, while the other would be down on the ground shoveling the dirt out by hand, both trying to get the grave dug and the deceased buried before the hole completely filled up with water. At some point, the shoveling was soupy mud. At some point the shovel would be set aside and both prisoners would use their hands to frantically try to get ahead of the water seepage. The grave always filled with water.

The coffins were made of cardboard, which would collapse under the weight of a grown man. The gravediggers usually knew the man they were trying to bury, so there was emotional attachment and personal transference of their own possible burial. The coffin was handled several times as the gravediggers would try to place it in the grave quicker than the water would accumulate. Eventually, the coffin would completely break apart, leaving them to drop the man and the broken cardboard container into the water-filled hole and just cover it up with dirt – and then deal with the engraved trauma of the day.

These types of experiences are difficult enough without the comments coming from uniformed on-lookers. They are even more difficult to bear whenever an indigent mother shows up at the graveside to say goodbye to her child and she witnesses the struggle born by the gravediggers and the absolute lack and detachment displayed by the state in his interment. And, the prisoners are not allowed to console the mother in any way. She stands alone, which is in extreme opposition to black culture - to human nature.

Climbing the Wall Moment

A couple of years ago our organization was granted funding to work with the children of the incarcerated. The project was a puppet show about having a parent in prison. The fifth and sixth graders wrote the script, made the puppets and the puppet theatre. They also created side shows of dance, song, rap, and drumming. The preparation and rehearsals spanned four months, twice weekly after school. These children were tightly wound and they struggled with "coloring within the lines." It was somewhat similar to trying to keep baby ducks in a shallow, overfull box. But, with the help of many devoted volunteers, interns, and staff, we managed to have a great performance. It was as if they had actually heard everything that we ever said to them, and somehow they all brought it to the stage at the same time – in front of two hundred people. That event was a miracle if I've ever seen one. But, what I want to talk about is a moment during a dance and song routine rehearsal. There were eight girls in the dance troupe. They had come up with the words and steps on their own and it was great. I had come into the room to observe and give final approval on the routine.

One of the main fifth-grade girls was doing everything but keeping step with the others. The best I could describe her movement is to say that she had the posture of a jumping jack and was smack against the wall, rolling around from her front to her back. I asked her to join the group, but she kept hugging the wall. I then got very short with her and brought tears to her eyes. I apologized but stressed that she needed to come into the rehearsal.

I was later telling her after-school teacher about it and that was when I learned that the girl's father had just gone off to prison, mom was on the streets, and the girl had been

moved into a new foster home the night
before, separate from her younger brother.

I am the one who is supposed to know
better. I'm the one who should understand
when a child literally climbs the wall. But, I
didn't. I forgot how difficult these children's
lives can be, and likely are. So, if I can so
easily fall into the forgetting, what about the
majority of the people who never have a
clue?

I found the girl the next week and apologized,
but that doesn't take the hurt back.

Uzi Moment

My co-facilitator in the grief and loss classes
recently shared one of his most intimate
experiences with the group. This came out
after having helped teach the class for three
years.

At the age of fourteen, he was riding the Los
Angeles streets with three other gang
members. He was in the back of the car
with his best friend. They were deeply
embedded in the gangster life of crime,
drugs, sex, and guns.

As the car was turning, a rival gang pulled
up and opened fire on the car with an uzi.
He was not hit, but he was covered with the
blood and flesh of his best friend, who was

shot in the head.

He went on to tell us that he went home, climbed into his bed, and no one could get him out of the bed for nearly three weeks. He kept the bloody clothes on because somehow it kept him from having to let go of his friend. He closed the story with "I was really messed up. He was my best friend. I don't talk about it."

Survivor's remorse is one of the most difficult traumas to process. In this case, he has been the survivor three times. His acting out has been equal to the impact of the traumas. In his case, prison probably did save his life. He is a rare anomaly - a model of how to use prison time to educate and rehabilitate oneself.

Poetry Moment

Ray Towler was incarcerated for thirty years for a crime that he did not commit. He was released, exonerated, and awarded a fortune that was supposed to make up for the injustice. Ray asked me to guide him as he reentered society, and to travel with him as he told his story through many international venues.

When I walked into our Slam Poetry class at Trumbull prison, about a month into Ray's release, my mind was fully occupied with the superinjustices that are widespread throughout America's court and penal systems.

I noticed a student I'd never seen before. He was a silver-haired black man, tall and slender. He was in a conversation with a couple of the other students when I entered the classroom. I watched as, one by one, the students entered the room and went directly to pay honor to this man. Who was he? I watched and listened. Then, I heard him mention he had recently been released from twenty-seven years in total isolation on death row. His innocence had been proven and he was preparing to be released.

At that point, I interrupted and asked if I had indeed heard him correctly. My next question was why he was in our class that morning. He gazed at me for a moment, smiled, and then softly told me he had been writing poetry and he wanted the pleasure of having an audience to recite it to. He had been invited into the class by the other students in his cell block.

I was honored to be in his audience. The poetry was all about love and what he missed most in life. I sat there. I sat there and pondered how a human can even live through so much isolation, injustice, and abuse. He was such a strong reminder that humans are, at their core, altruistic and caring. Like Ray, he had his freedom wrongfully ripped from him, and had lost three decades to incarceration. But, this man had been totally isolated and any contact he had had with other human beings for those twenty-seven years had been cruel and abusive. All negative, he told me. He stayed after class and told me his history. It was horrible.

Where I was still struggling to wrap my mind and heart around Ray's reality, I realized he had at least lived in the general population with other prisoners and people. All of a sudden I was overwhelmed with the realization that the depth of injustice is far more than I am capable of imagining or emotionally surviving. And these are just two examples out of thousands that scream in the night - not every prisoner is guilty! Our justice system - just isn't!

Conclusion

Prisoners are people too. People – not economic units. Prisons should promote human values rather than destroy them. If we can't help people to realize their own universal value - that they are a divine creation interwoven within the fabric, the whole of life - how can we expect them to see the value in their victims or their environment? This is gained through asset building, not punitive action. Government needs to stop making justice decisions based on economic units. We need alternatives to prison.

We need meaningful reentry programs that are rooted in social entrepreneurship, healthy family units, and mentoring. The mentoring must be patient and recognize that individuals who have studied personal and social change in the vacuum of incarceration have not had opportunities to practice that knowledge in normal social groups and relationships. The individuals often experience confusion and struggle as they find their way through the application process. They have to make the journey from parroting rhetoric of their studies to the active realization of applying cognitive behavior in a very conscious and balanced manner. They must further recognize and resist the tendency to habitually react in former emotional and volitional patterns. This is the five-hundred pound gorilla that often travels with individuals on the reentry journey. A huge clue to successful reentry is the individual's willingness to be open to talking about the gorilla and to engage others in their mental and emotional journey. This is contra to the hidden rules of prison life.

Society constructs the self. We as a society must recognize and actively invest in correcting the atrocious traumas that drive anger, violence and crime – and poverty. We share the scars. We share the responsibility of our nation's future. It takes community to reduce recidivism. It takes community to create thriving families.

REFERENCE LIST

Amerine, Phil, Dowdell, John (2009).
Developing Problem-solving Strategies for
Successful Reentry.
  Elkridge, MD: Correctional
  Education Association

Briney, Carol E. (2012). Prison Coffee Table
Book Project Vol 1, Edition 2.
  Canton, Ohio: Reentry Bridge
  Network, Inc.

Briney, Carol E. (2012). Prison Coffee Table
Book Project Vol 2, Edition 2.
  Canton, Ohio: Reentry Bridge
  Network, Inc.

Briney, Carol E. (2012). The Retablo Affect,
Edition 2. Canton, Ohio: Reentry Bridge
Network, Inc.

Collins, Terry J. (2007). The Reentry
Movement in Corrections: Shift in Paradigm
or Passing Fad?
  Corrections Today, April 2007, page 8.

Damon, Matt, Affleck, Ben (1997). Goodwill
Hunting, screenplay: Gus Van Sant, Director.

Ford, Debbie (2001). The Secret of the Shadow: The Power of Owning Your Whole Story.
New York, NY: HarperCollins Publishers.

Haney, C., Banks, W.C. & Zimbardo, P.G. (1973). A study of prisoners and guards in a simulated prison.
Naval Research Review, 30, 4-17.

Harvey, Steve (2011). Act Like a Lady, Think Like a Man: What Men Really Think About Love, Relationships, Intimacy, and Commitment.
New York, NY: HarperCollins Publishers.

James, John W., Friedman, Russell (2009). The Grief Recovery Handbook, 20th Anniversary Expanded Edition.
New York, NY: Harper Collins Publishers.

Howard, Michael L. (2008). Children Who Have Been Traumatized: One Court's Response.
Juvenile and Family Court Journal, Volume 59, Issue 4, pages 21–34, Fall 2008. Retrieved from http://onlinelibrary.wiley.com doi/10.1111/j.1755 6988.2008.00019.x/abstract

Payne, Ruby K. (2005). <u>A Framework for Understanding Poverty, Edition 4</u>.
Highlands, TX: aha! Process, Inc.

Ramsey, Dave (2012). <u>Financial Peace University</u>. Brentwood, TN: Lampo Licensing, LLC.

Schwartz, Robert (2009). <u>Your Soul's Plan: Discovering the Real Meaning of the Life You Planned Before You Were Born</u>.
Berkeley, CA: Frog Books, North Atlantic Books.

Shea, Christopher (2012). Why Power Corrupts. <u>Smithsonian Magazine</u>, October 2012. Retrieved from
<u>http://www.smithsonianmag.com/ science-nature/Why-Power- Corrupts-169804606.html</u>

Steele, William (2013). <u>Working with Grieving & Traumatized Children & Adolescents: Discovering What Matters Most Through Evidence-Based, Sensory Interventions.</u>
Canada: John Wiley & Sons